REFLECTIONS
an autobiographical journey

Also by Paul Cox

Home of Man, the People of New Guinea, with Ulli Beier
Human Still Lives from Nepal
Mirka, with Ulli Beier
I Am, with Wim Cox
Three Screenplays:
　Lonely Hearts
　My First Wife
　A Woman's Tale

REFLECTIONS
an autobiographical journey

paul cox

Currency Press • Sydney

First published in 1998 by
Currency Press Pty Ltd,
PO Box 2287, Strawberry Hills,
NSW 2012, Australia

Copyright © Paul Cox 1998

This book is copyright. Apart from any fair dealing for the purpose of private study, research or review, as permitted under the Copyright Act, no part may be reproduced by any process without written permission. Inquiries concerning reproduction, publication, translation or recording rights should be addressed to the publishers.

NATIONAL LIBRARY OF AUSTRALIA CIP DATA

Cox, Paul, 1940-.
Reflections.

Includes index.
ISBN 0 86819 549 9.

1. Cox, Paul, 1940-. 2. Motion picture producers and directors — Australia — Biography. 3. Motion picture industry — Australia. 4. Motion pictures — Production and direction — Australia. I. Title.

791.430233092

Book design by Eye Visuals
Printed in Australia by Star Printery Pty Ltd, Sydney

Contents

Introduction	7
Glimpses of my Youth in a Provincial Dutch Town on the German Border	11
Leaving Home	53
A New Beginning	75
India	90
The United States	113
Dreams, Stories and Magic Moments	130
Friends, Foes and Some Chronological Order	149
A Woman's Tale, The Nun and the Bandit, Exile, Lust and Revenge	170
The Children	192
Filmography	210
Retrospectives	217
Index	219

FOR EZRA, KYRA AND MARIUS

I wish to thank Margot Wiburd and Leonie Verhoeven for their tireless efforts in deciphering my handwriting and helping me to distinguish between the truths and untruths, between the memories, the madness and the dreams. I must also thank the poets, whose words have inspired me and helped me to see.

Introduction

As a growing boy in my home town I was a member of a post-war street-gang that had worked out a perfect system for going to the movies. One of us would buy a ticket to which we all contributed. He or she would then go inside, open the back door and let everyone in. How we got away with this is still as mysterious to me as the films we saw. I don't remember any of them, have no recollection at all of what happened on the big screen. The only thing I remember very clearly was the 'absolute nature of the image'. How was it possible to cover a whole wall with a moving picture and make the other walls disappear?

One day this cinema had to make way for a supermarket — like most of our treasured places nowadays — and my interest in the medium vanished. I was more or less forced to become a photographer and nothing related to film stirred in me, until much later.

In foreign cities I always look for good movies. Usually there are one or two, but often they play in obscure suburban cinemas way out of town. So I spend my time in bookshops or music shops looking for books on film — not the 'Golden Years of Hollywood' type that celebrate the stars or worship the box-office but books by people who understand and love the cinema. Unfortunately this search for books written by the artists of the cinema is as frustrating as the search for good films. There is simply not much good material available. One finds at least a hundred cook books to one book on film, yet most people spend much more time watching television than cooking or eating. It's the same with poetry books. Nobody buys books on poetry, yet poetry is everywhere. It seems only logical to me that people should be more interested in what goes on behind the screen. After all, the moving image has a much more powerful influence on their lives than the latest cooking trends.

Book publishers are very much like film distributors. In their frantic search for instant hits they usually bypass what is imaginative and new. God help all those unpublished authors who write about the light but remain in the dark.

A writer friend assures me that publishers are worse than film distributors and that I should not expect these 'reflections' to be published in this form. Well, so be it. I would never have continued to make films if I had accepted the verdict of the 'experts', if I had allowed myself to doubt my faith in the individual.

Poetic justice does exist somehow, the world has a conscience that in the end cannot be bribed — publishers and distributors with vision do exist. A rare breed of heroes who realise their responsibility and are motivated by their sense of adventure and commitment. They know that if man has a future at all, this future lies in man's ability to be creative and to develop his natural ability to be compassionate, and not just in the worship of science and reason.

To understand or explain the so-called creative process, however, is an impossible task. The legacy Vincent van Gogh left behind is probably as close as we can get to some understanding of what goes on in the head of a true artist. His writings travel very closely together with his paintings. In the most powerful words, he explains what went on during '... the production of some canvases that will retain their calm even in the catastrophe'.

As he moves on, Vincent's questions become more refined, surer, and though broken in health and spirit he has gone full circle by the time he kills himself. The suicide comes as no surprise to anyone who has studied his life closely.

Vincent somehow manages to share his illuminations, his 'glimpses of the light' with us. He's totally honest about his life and his thoughts and has the rare ability, through language, to give his feelings form and shape. Language only expresses what we think, yet because the ability to think is very much part of our conditioning, language usually makes us say the wrong thing in the right way and only hints at our 'inner reality'.

There's something in our collective psyche that fortunately rejects the here and now and searches for a larger truth.

To express what we feel requires a total detachment from all we know, because feeling and thinking are diametrically opposed. I believe that the emotional man must dominate the intelligent one. This must be the case otherwise there can be no music, no hope, no natural confusion and no tenderness. In van Gogh's earlier letters there's a marvellous passage about his awakening to light and how his abolition of conventional methods allowed him to scream out: 'I'm so glad I've never learned painting.'

Everything we do must somehow be a self-portrait — not to please or reflect the ego, but to nourish our ability to share beauty and to reflect our inner truths. As Oscar Wilde said, 'Everything made with feeling is a portrait of the maker, not of the subject.'

Many events of the past have wormed their way into my films and breathed life into them. They are important now in terms of the new shape they have found. Therefore I need to write a little about my youth, so that I can continue the journey with more detachment from the past.

When I was about four, German soldiers marched into the house.

Glimpses of my Youth in a Provincial Dutch Town on the German Border

'Through the evening mist — our youth, half solid, half composed of dreams ...'

My first memory goes back to a rainy day in Holland. The city in ruins. My mother pushes an old pram through the rubble. Black planes dance through the skies. My brother and I hide in the pram. I am three years of age. My mother parks us in front of the bakery and goes inside. With his legs my brother starts to push me against the side of the pram. I cannot escape and scream for help. As soon as my mother comes running, my brother stops. My mother does not understand why I am so frightened. It is only when she holds me tightly that this feeling of total helplessness vanishes. A few hours later the sun breaks through the clouds. We play in the sand close to our home. Suddenly day turns into night. Thousands of planes flying closely together cover the sky like a giant bird in charge of the light. For the rest of the day I hold my mother's hand for fear of being left alone in that sudden darkness.

Our border town suffered more or less the same fate as Dresden, except that the planes and the sirens went on and on for the first five years of my life. No wonder I still feel slightly nervous when more than one plane crosses the sky or when I see the ingenuity of modern warfare.

Years later this story emerged.

The beach was black, deserted. In front of me a large, solid bridge — one pole in the sand supporting a huge pattern of iron lace. The bridge stretched as far as my eyes could see across the oily sea. The harsh sun sat low on the horizon. My shadow was a glittering mass of tiny fishes on the sand. Suddenly a real shadow spread across the sky and covered me in darkness. The sound of aeroplanes could be heard and I saw thousands of big black birds flying closely together, obscuring the sun. Slowly the birds merged into one and an enormous bird with the head of an old man landed in front of me. His long grey hair gradually turned into feathers. His teeth were sparkling diamonds. The sand slowly turned into a soft, sliding substance. I felt myself sinking into the deep, my legs merging, then becoming one with the sand. A blind fear came over me as the bird grabbed my hair and lifted my head far up into the sky. From high above I could see the shadow of my body on the sand. Only the head was missing.

There were other war events that shaped my life.

When I was about four, German soldiers marched into our house. I knew that my uncle had been hiding in a kitchen cabinet, but had fortunately moved elsewhere that morning. The soldiers went berserk and kicked in every door and cabinet they could find. From my height, their black boots flashing past my face had an unforgettably menacing and evil impact. I'm still wary of people in boots and wear sandals on all occasions.

A week later we were evacuated to the north of Holland. The

journey went via Germany. We had to walk for many kilometres. The road to the train will never be forgotten. The German army was fleeing and the British army tried to halt the retreat. Bombs exploded everywhere around us. People dived in and out of trenches. A woman behind me was decapitated. A speeding truck with German soldiers tried to drive us off the road. The madness, bravery and cowardice of these people who were trying to save themselves still lingers. Miraculously, our family survived. My two elder sisters were terrified, but my brother and I were too young to comprehend the dangers and watched the fireworks with a degree of fascination. My father was sick and my poor mother ran from one to another to comfort us. We were helpless refugees forced to recognise the authority of brutality and death.

I was wearing five pairs of trousers and seven jumpers, like a Michelin puppet. We couldn't carry much, so my mother had dressed us in just about everything we possessed. We were hungry and exhausted. An aunt who had come with us threw herself in front of a truck and was pulled on board by screaming soldiers. She was warned that the truck contained ammunition and could be blown up at any moment. Later that night she returned with a few loaves of bread and a jar of jam. She was weeping and looked distraught. My father said my aunt had saved our lives.

We were locked in large train carriages like cattle going to the slaughterhouse. The story of the three-day journey is gruesome; many suffocated or died of starvation. I don't remember much of it, only the wailing of a woman whose husband had died in her arms. Her cries pierced my ears, my bones and my heart.

I've never understood why we make films about war. Most of these films glamorise aspects of war and often celebrate their heroes for the wrong reasons. War heroes and movie heroes are difficult to separate. Maybe it's better to avoid heroes altogether on the big screen.

For six months we lived in the north of Holland. My mother had made suits out of felt that made it hard to move or run, but protected us against the bitter cold. We stayed in a farm near a small village. I found more warmth amongst the cows in the stable than amongst the people with whom we were staying. On Liberation Day large tanks appeared on the road leading into the village. They were too heavy for the road and left a trail of smashed concrete behind. A soldier threw me some lollies, which I gratefully accepted. I had never tasted a sweet.

When we returned after the war, we found that another family had moved into our house. We were forced to share the home with them. Why were these people living in our house as if it were their home? They spoke a strange dialect from the north and argued loudly throughout the day. Once a week a representative from the local church would come to check on us. Everyone would put on their best behaviour and pretend things were fine, but living with the other family became impossible. I remember the tension very well, although names and faces have vanished. How could there be such anger and frustration amongst these people who had survived the war? It came to the point where one of the families had to move out, but which family and where would they go? This was left in the hands of the almighty Church and a young, rosy-cheeked priest was dispatched to sort out the mess. My father, who was either silent or extremely cynical, lost his temper with him and threatened to throw him out. The poor man fled through the back door and alarmed his superiors. The bishop himself ordered both fathers to appear at a special tribunal. The outcome was in my father's favour. The other family left in absolute silence and, according to my father, stole as much as they could before disappearing. One of the few toys I possessed, an old wooden puppet, was taken by one of the children. I didn't care much about it, but pretended to have suffered a big loss. My false tears were noticed, which made me feel

*1944 in the north of Holland with my mother
and brother Wim wearing our 'felt suits'.*

part of the general disgust and my usual dreadful feeling of inferiority from not being able to express myself disappeared momentarily.

It was a difficult time for my parents; my mother was pregnant again and my father was looking for another profession with which to make a living. As a filmmaker he knew enough about photography to make a start, so with the help of the Church, my father started a photographic studio called 'Studio 45'. We never found out why he called it 'Studio 45'. The most logical explanation was that he started it in 1945, but when confronted with this interpretation, he strongly denied that the date had anything to do with it. There was something more to it … much more. Unfortunately he could never tell us what. He loved secrecy, especially when it had no substance.

In the first five years of my life I witnessed nothing but death and destruction. I was always immensely relieved to come home and find the house still standing. People regularly disappeared and everything always turned into rubble. For the next five years I walked through the ruins of our town and played in dangerous building sites. That continuous sense of loss left a passion for old structures and I always feel a deep personal guilt when an old building is pulled down. Every time a road was repaired, we'd test it with our treasured old car tyres, rolling them over the bitumen. A flat surface was so new, so unfamiliar. Even now, when I walk into a hotel with a shiny marble floor I hesitate and take a few tentative steps. To walk on flat marble is still a great luxury.

One sunny afternoon the Red Cross parked a van right in the middle of the church square. Hot chocolate and biscuits were distributed amongst the population. It was the first time in my life that I had experienced the taste of hot chocolate. What an extraordinary delight it was! Rich, creamy, almost edible. What luxury! Hot chocolate, to me, is still a sacred drink. I enjoy it on very rare occasions.

Then my school days started. On the first day my mother took

1946, my brother Wim and I at School.

me into the classroom and wept openly when I let go of her hand. I was seated next to the butcher's son. There was a stove in the middle of the room with a long pipe running across the roof to a hole in the ceiling. On the walls, various charts with coloured slogans: '*Zeg Mies, zeem jij de ruit voor moe*'[1] and '*Wat kan Paultje toch mooi zingen*'.[2] These were going to help us with our spelling. The teacher's name was Miss Schouren, a woman with a sour face but a kind heart. From the very first day I developed a strange fascination with her bosom. I felt deeply sorry for her ... why those bumps in front? Why couldn't she be like other people? Like men, for instance. Admittedly my mother's bosom also worried me greatly, but she was my mother and mothers were meant to have bosoms. Nevertheless I felt sorry for her too.

When a large aunt with even larger breasts came to visit, I was convinced that she had put them on for the occasion. This could not be real! I shyly observed her from a distance until my mother asked me to pass her a cup of coffee. I eagerly responded. With trembling hands I offered her the cup. In total fascination I watched closely as she drank it. When she had finished I wanted to take the cup from her, but my hand somehow did not obey me and slipped into her dress. My father tried to usher me away but my hand somehow got stuck and had to be forcefully removed. I still remember the immense softness of her flesh and the sudden dizziness that made me almost faint.

Some time later my mother's sister came to stay with us. She came from East Germany and had been very cruel to my mother when they were both little girls, so my mother told us. Here was somebody to watch, to be wary of. This woman had a cruel nature. I found her very beautiful, though. The fact that she came from

---

[1] '*Hey Mies, are you cleaning the window for mum?*'
[2] '*How come little Paul can sing so beautifully?*'

another country and spoke a different language fascinated me.

I watched her wash her hands. I watched her dry them. She smelled strange to me, very strange. What was it? Her odour took over the whole house. Nobody else noticed. Did it come from her bosom? I would not let her out of my sight. The urge to smell her close by became unbearable. Finally I forced my nose into her thigh and had to be severely smacked to come back to my senses.

The flashbacks in *Man of Flowers* are largely based upon these encounters. Flashbacks are memories, frozen in an eternal solid form, so concentrated that no distortion is possible.

I used to sleepwalk at regular intervals. My mother was terrified that I might fall out of the window, or hurt myself in my wanderings through the night. To wake up in another room or stand on a table had a strange impact. It felt as if someone else was possessing my body and moving me about. In my dreams I sometimes recall this feeling.

One night my parents found me in the kitchen, standing on a chair with a large knife in my hands. My father managed to disarm me and put me back to bed. I remember very clearly that I was totally conscious of everything, my mother's panic and my father's anger, but I couldn't wake up or indicate in any way to my parents that I knew what was going on.

The sleepwalking ceased as I grew older and was replaced by a dreadful vagueness that used to infuriate my father. Once I made three trips to the local tobacconist to buy him some cigars. The first time I forgot what to buy. The second time I purchased a packet of cigarettes instead. On my final trip I got the cigars all right, but put the box in a bookcase at home and could not remember where I had put them.

My father had built a darkroom on the third floor. The living room was turned into a studio. A long cord hung between the banisters, attached to an old bicycle bell. One pull was for the coffee break, two pulls for his dinner and three pulls for the phone, which was downstairs. As business improved the telephone rang more often and my father's journeys up and down the stairs increased. Maybe it would have been possible to put an extension phone upstairs, but this way we could all witness the fact that my father was working for his family. He called it slaving!

My mother, meanwhile, had given birth to another child, a girl. They called her Angeline. This was her fifth child. There was still another daughter to come.

One day my father found the time to take me for a walk. For some reason we went on our own. Not far from the house were the woods with small farms scattered all around. My father warned me that the further we went, the longer the trip home, so I had to be tough and stand up to it. At the edge of the town we found a small creek with many fishes and large dragonflies. A tiny bridge with peeling paint. Then we entered the forest. How soft that carpet of green on which we walked. How dark those large, mysterious trees. My father kept explaining things to me. Every bird, every tree had a name. I wanted him to be silent.

I remember the soft wind, the birds, the clouds and especially the light. Everything so dark, so mysterious. Then suddenly, a strong shaft of light when the sun burned through the clouds. It illuminated the forest, penetrated the soil, took my breath away. Deep down I felt that I was witnessing something very special that would never leave me. The final words Sheila Florance speaks in *A Woman's Tale* are literally taken from this experience and the discovery of that light. Also in *Cactus* Isabelle Huppert as Colo recalls that 'sudden light in the forest' as she realises her sight is fading.

*Wim Cox and Else Cox-Kuminack.
'I think they were happy until the war started.'*

When we returned from the forest, my father told my mother that I had stood up well to the walk and was a big boy now. My dear mother pressed my face against her heart. It was the first time that I perceived a glimpse of her mortality.

Thirty-eight years later my father and I went to visit my mother's grave. As we walked through the local cemetery, a soft hill of green appeared in the distance, surrounded by a row of enormous trees. I expected my mother to be buried there, but my father turned a corner and pointed at her grave. A small patch of soil amongst others — it was the wrong spot! Suddenly I was seven years old again, totally thrown by the enormity of life and death. I almost reached out to hold his hand, then looked at his face. Tears, endless tears streamed down the heavy lines of his skin. Now I was the father and he the child. My heart stopped with grief, 'that great grief of human life'. In a flash every tree, every sound in the forest returned. I waited for that shaft of light to burn through the trees, but found no new light and plunged into the dark. My father's face was ashen. The wind stirred his greyness, his eyes wept. A small printed line read: 'Else Amalia Cox-Kuminack'. My mother, my very own mother, was dead.

Ever since my departure from Europe, the impending death of my mother had haunted me. Of course, most of our mothers are special. But she was a great human being who gave to anyone who needed it. She did not know how to take; consequently she was exploited by my father, by her children, by virtually all who knew and loved her.

When I lived away from Europe, a relationship with her blossomed that was of great comfort to me. She was always there, larger than life. I owe all my humanity to her. Erwin Rado, a dear friend and for many years the director of the Melbourne Film Festival, told me a

My mother before she left Germany.

few years before his death: 'I've always missed my mother. How can anyone live without his mother?' Erwin was seventy at the time.

Else Kuminack was born in Germany. Her mother, a fine looking aristocratic woman with a French background. Her father, a stern man with a large moustache. German, Polish, Hungarian. Both her parents died when she was sixteen. Else made her way to Holland and became *au pair* to the children of a Dutch baron who lived in a large castle on the outskirts of a small village. Those children remained close to her all her life.

One day Wim Cox arrived with a small film crew. His own father was the director of a publishing house and had helped him and his brother Henk to start a film company. The films they made were humourless but skilful and inventive. Else found him charming and intelligent, and admired his 'obsessive sense of perfection'. He took her for drives in his old Ford and taught her how to use a movie camera. Within a few weeks they were in love and decided to marry. Their wedding was celebrated by the whole village. Photographs show a brass band serenading the happy couple, with many bridesmaids standing on the steps of the castle. I think they were happy until the war started.

The only real sin my mother ever committed was that she loved her children more than her husband. My father never recovered from the war years. Grew bitter and cold. Our childhood was steeped in great misery. It was only after my parents had grown old and grey that some peace came to them.

It's hard to recall the despair of my lost, old, unhappy youth. Sometimes when I visit my sisters and brother we sit in helpless silence, trying to forget.

When my daughter Kyra was born, I swore that I would try to give her a happy youth, that she would not suffer the same deathly loneliness and despair that made it so difficult for me to find myself later on in life. That terrible battle between what I was and what I should have been, according to my father. Children have the capacity to feel totally, and injustice and insensitivity scar them for life.

As we were not 'working class', my chances of being called upon to join the ranks of altar boys were high. Indeed, one fine day my parents were informed of my potential and they had no option but to offer my services to the Church. My elder brother Wim's career as an altar boy was already flourishing. His incense pot flew higher than anyone else's. His Latin was impeccable, his altar manners mature and discreet. A difficult image to live up to. Nobody, however, recognised that Wim suffered from a rare somnambulant imbalance. One morning his incense pot flew off into the vestry, almost killing a young priest. A few days later he dropped the mass book. The next day he dozed off during a service and literally fell off his pedestal. Our family name was severely disgraced. My poor brother was put on stand-by and it hung upon my fragile shoulders to repair the damage.

As altar boys we had to kneel down for hours on the cold, hard marble and carry the mass book, or take the wine to the right spot at exactly the right moment. To remain alert and awake during these endless celebrations was quite a challenge; I learned about the many dimensions of time. The endless repetitive rituals of the Catholic Mass extended one hour well beyond my comprehension.

On my first communion, my godfather had given me a watch: a black watch with green fluorescent numbers and a tiny hand for seconds. The brand name 'Andora' did not light up in the dark but everything else did. During these services that watch hardly moved — even the small hand for seconds seemed paralysed. I would change the mass book, hold my breath for a while, stare at the ceiling, then slowly peep at the watch. Hours had gone by, yet the watch had only registered thirty or forty seconds.

In the middle of the mass, the altar boys were allowed to sit back and pay attention to the weekly sermon. Our pastor was a direct representative of the Good Lord and was consequently treated with enormous respect and adulation. He would start quietly and lovingly, bless everyone and everything in sight and then slowly become angry, very angry. Sometimes he would focus on individual faces that had probably given away their finest secrets during confession, then bombard them with God's scorn.

We, the lost sheep, were guilty, guilty of life, guilty of death, guilty of all sufferings. When he had exhausted himself and literally blown enough spit into the congregation to drench the people in front, he would slowly return to his quiet, peaceful, loving self and continue the service. The people's collective guilt would hang low — low enough for the money collectors to drain the guilty clouds. The pastor himself lived in a large, dark house, adjourning the church. His ancient housekeeper spent her days cleaning the many windows, eyeing the passers-by with suspicion and envy. She was called 'the dragon'.

At school the most important daily event was one hour of religious instruction. God was the creator of all, had actually made everything, including us children. All we had to do was believe in God and his creations. It was that easy. That all-embracing, important question: 'Why are we on earth?' was also easily answered. 'To serve God and thus find a place in heaven'. We should never ask too many questions. That would only cause confusion and lead to dangerous temptations. One wrong move or thought could disappoint God and we would be punished. The trouble was that nobody had ever seen God. How could they be so sure about God, if he'd never been spotted anywhere? For several weeks I pondered this question. When I finally gathered enough courage to confront our pastor in the dark of the confession box, I was told: 'God is everywhere and in order to love him, he has to be concealed from view.' People weren't capable of dealing with the real presence of God. The moment he showed himself, we'd stop loving him. But why ask this question? This is not what God asks from us. He gave me a large penance. God was also definitely male. That's why females were not allowed to cross the altar or walk into the vestry.

Then there was the Virgin birth. According to the priests, a virgin was someone rare and noble, an example of the highest purity in the land. There was a bit of logic missing somewhere. Joseph was the father of Jesus and yet not his biological father. Jesus' real father was God himself, but Jesus himself was also God. Then there was the Holy Ghost to complete the picture. Here we had a triangle of three separate Gods that were supposed to be taken as one. The Holy Ghost? What was his contribution? Where did he come from? Did he have something to do with the immaculate conception? I had enormous trouble coping with this, but didn't dare ask any more questions.

Now I wish the word 'God' — or love, for that matter — didn't exist. Then we would be free to discover for ourselves who God is and what love is.

Meanwhile my brother Wim, being a creative spirit, was forced to concentrate more on his theatrical activities. Amateur theatre was thriving amongst the population. One fine night he played two characters, an angel and a wolf, in a play that had obviously been conceived locally. It had too many strange twists to be understood anywhere else in the world. To change out of the angel's costume — including halo — and creep into the wolf's outfit was not an easy task and the time allowed was extremely short. When he reappeared as the wolf, God bless his soul, the audience of proud parents with their offspring, exploded. His wolf's mask was facing the right way, but he had put the costume on the wrong way around. A long tail was hanging in front. Mary, Jesus' mother, also a character in the play, quickly tried to snap the tail off to save further embarrassment, but to no avail. This caused such hilarity amongst the audience that the curtain had to be dropped and further performances cancelled. My poor brother hid indoors for many days. They were after his blood.

Some time later, he reappeared in a minor play called *The Prince of Orange*. He modestly played the lead. On the first night everything went extremely well. A comeback seemed possible. But the next night when a servant — played by me — came on stage with a message that the Prince of Habsburg had died, he confused this with his own part and read out loudly: 'The Prince of Orange has died!.' One of my sisters, playing a Princess of Orange, became hysterical with laughter and urinated all over the stage. She had to be escorted into the wings.

I tried to save my brother's career and whispered: 'It's not the Prince of Orange ...That's you ... It's the Prince of Habsburg who's died'. I shall never forget the helpless look on my brother's face when his mouth refused to respond to his brain and he said: 'A mistake has been made ... it's not the Prince of Habsburg who's died, but the Prince of Orange'. My sister had another loud attack from the wings and two more members of the cast screamed off the stage, leaving a trail of urine behind. Wim still hadn't noticed his mistake, but it was obvious that his acting career had come to a grinding halt.

Reality is not only stranger than fiction, it's also much funnier. To put this on film is the ultimate challenge. Why is this so difficult?

I think those early years after the war were quite happy. People were rebuilding their lives and had little time to waste on silly matters. Life itself was appreciated. Every dinner was a banquet,

One of our school plays, My brother plays Maria and I appear as an angel second from right.

every outing a holiday. For a long time the war was never mentioned. The regular sirens of the bomb disposal units were ignored. Those who had crawled from under the ruins picked up the old threads and went full blast into this business of living.

Then an aunt of my mother's died. My mother went to the funeral in Belgium and after her return we often found her in a corner, weeping inconsolably. This aunt had had three sons. One after the other they had died during the war: one in combat, one in jail and the last and youngest son tortured to death by the Germans. Three years after the war her heart gave way from grief. She had cried every day from morn 'til night. Her last words were: 'My sons never harmed a soul.' One of her sons had been a poet, the other a fine musician and the last a promising painter. They were artists!

The way my mother recalled the pain of her aunt had an enormous impact on me — 'She died from grief', haunted me for years. In *Island* Irene Papas says these very words. I stood, deeply moved, behind the camera when Irene made these words real again.

Slowly other stories emerged. My father had been taken to hospital with a stomach perforation. The operation was delayed due to a lack of staff. He was given the last rites and after my mother had sat with him all night, she returned home to be with her children. She was asked to come back as soon as possible, as they did not expect my father to live.

My mother walked home through the devastated city and realised with horror that part of our street had been destroyed overnight. Like a mad woman she ran through the ruins to find her children. When she found us in a neighbour's cellar, she screamed and cried for hours. I was the youngest and from then on she carried me wherever she went. Every day she took me to the hospital on her back. When my father started to recover, he painted a large mural on the walls of the hospital: dark trees with a pond, a flock of birds and red clouds. The clouds were bleeding, he said.

I have always had a great respect for people who create something out of nothing. That certainly includes the baker and the carpenter, but I have my doubts about the butcher.

Four weeks after the war started, when I was five weeks old, my mother took me to the window of the large house in which I was born. A battle had taken place in the park down below. Dead soldiers were lying amongst the trees, on the bridge across the water and floating in the pond. My mother covered my eyes with her hands, scared that something might register. She was ashamed of the world she'd brought me into, she said. I still fantasise about this image and sometimes rearrange the bodies in the park. On the rare occasions that I return to the place of my birth, I feel more drawn to this house than the house I remember. It helps me to recollect my mother's memories. They're clear and alive in my mind, like she is.

More than half a century later a strange thing happened. Leonie Verhoeven, a Dutch student of the cinema, watched the BBC one night and saw my film *Cactus*. She was touched by it and went looking for other films I'd made. When I made an appearance at the Film Festival in Utrecht, she realised that my background was Dutch and decided to do her thesis on my films. Someone put her in touch with my sister Angeline. The next time I visited Holland, Leonie came to meet me. She brought me a small present. It was an old postcard she'd found in a shop — a photograph taken in Venlo, the town of my birth. Here was the park with the pond and the bridge, taken from below the window where my mother had shown me the world for the first time. On the back a short message with an address and the date of posting. The postcard had been posted three days before my birth. After checking with a retired postmaster in Holland, I realised that the postcard had arrived on the very day of my birth.

Apart from the fact that there were no dead bodies, this was the picture that had haunted me for so long. Here, right in front of me, a real link with the past — alive with the mysterious seeds of *Man of Flowers*. Leonie knew that I was born in Venlo, hence this gift, but that was all. 'Why this particular image?' 'It reminded me of your films', she said.

I'm recalling this in transit at the airport in Tokyo. When I left Amsterdam and the customs officer looked at my passport, he said: 'Ah, born in Venlo ... me too.' Then he started to talk to me in the local dialect, which is a strange mixture of German and medieval Dutch. It left me totally dumbfounded.

As I grow older early events of my youth reappear more frequently and with greater clarity. Strange, irrelevant observations flash through the mind like arrows, then suddenly find meaning. Memories, dreams and visions float into one, become one.

On my first visit to Nepal, I hired a small rowing boat which took me out onto Lake Pokahra. I had no idea that the lake was close to one of the highest mountains in the world, the Annapurna. The sky was soft and overcast. I closed my eyes and slipped into that hypnotic threshold between sleep and consciousness. When I looked up, the clouds had drifted apart and exposed the mountain, 'half solid, half composed of dreams'. It didn't really register. I thought that the clouds had formed a castle in the sky. I closed my eyes again and climbed the mountain, along small dirt tracks made my way to the highest peak. From high above I saw myself drifting on the water. Then I awoke and again the mountain was exposed for a few seconds. This could only exist in my mind. It was too beautiful. It started to rain. I made my way back to the shore, felt strangely blessed and holy. The next day when the sky was clear and blue and the Annapurna rose in all its glory above the village, I realised I'd seen a real mountain in the sky and that I'd conquered it.

The postcard of the Venlo park.

In Tel Aviv I saw an old man whose body was so bent that his face almost touched the footpath. He still managed to walk and convene with a little dog at his side. The dog was followed by three other dogs, all marching in line, controlled by a strange, inner discipline. Then I remembered a man in the war who had been rounded up by the Germans and forced to march down the road to be shot, his hands on his neck, his face well down. The soldiers behind him walked like these dogs in line. Disciplined killers, controlled by an outside, more destructive force.

In the south of France I stayed in an almost derelict, mould-ridden hotel run by an old woman dressed in black. Every morning, descending the endless staircase, one could smell the coffee this woman had waiting for us. Slowly one became immersed in something so familiar and yet so ancient, that it seemed as if all the coffee houses in the world had opened their doors. To finally drink the coffee from large bowls full of cracks and missing handles was immensely satisfying. I have such a vivid recollection of this that even now, many years later, as soon as the smell of coffee hits me, the atmosphere of this place returns with all its intimacy and detail.

Yet our imagination at times plays tricks with our memories. Our dreams invade our truths. It is difficult to write about the past without distorting certain facts. It took quite a few years until a general preoccupation with the war took hold of the population of our town. Monuments were erected, plaques unveiled, new holidays invented. People tried to come to terms with the horrific truth of the war. Initially they had been too stunned. Some strange, mystical moments surfaced. One night we all went outside and saw a big cross standing in a full moon. A large ball of fire entered a window of the cellar in which we were sleeping, engulfed us all in light, then disappeared without a trace. A bullet hole appeared in a window right in front of me and should have pierced my forehead. The bullet was never found.

Maybe these stories emerged from dreams, but each member of

my family would vow that all this really happened. Years later I started to realise that my roots were planted in some other land, some other time. I dream of large fields of flowers, meadows of green, of endless laneways with slender trees, of dirt tracks in the mountains. I dream, I dream, I dream.

An incident that shook my early life needs to be mentioned. Queen Wilhelmina of the Netherlands, with her entourage, had decided to honour our town with a visit. A special toilet was erected for the occasion at a cost of five hundred guilders. Everybody discussed the high cost of the toilet, but I was deeply disappointed to discover that the Queen needed to use the toilet like anybody else. The kids at school joked about it, but I was shocked.

On the big day, we were all marched down the road and strategically positioned so that the Queen could see us and we could see her. It was bitterly cold. With frozen hands we practised how to wave our little paper flags. A brass band played the National Anthem non-stop. Now and then an announcement about the approaching Mother of the Nation. She was badly delayed. In hastily erected tents, frozen hands and feet were put back into operation. I had also lost hold of my little flag and was ushered into the tent to be rescued. Suddenly applause and excited voices. I stormed out of the tent to see my Queen, but she had already sped past and disappeared into the distance. After hours of misery, I had missed her. It was too much for me. The awful truth would not sink in, however. I still raised my flag and kept waving until people started to laugh. I felt deeply humiliated and wouldn't speak to anyone for days.

Now I search my mind for other events. Minor or major. The minor ones are usually the most important ones. The daily walk to school past the school hedge. Who lived behind that hedge? The street corner where we were forced to hold hands before crossing.

The neighbour's dog which tore a small dog to pieces in front of our very eyes. The always smiling Chinaman who walked the streets selling peanuts. Although he scared us a little, I always envied him his freedom. His name was Peanut Bill and he was much despised and ill-treated by the 'burghers' of our town. Some forty years later his unique independence became too much for the town's collective guilt; now they have erected a small statue in honour of this outcast. Close to the centre 'Pindawilliam' reigns on a pedestal, watching the eager shoppers who once again ignore him in passing.

The games my brother played with his friends that excluded me. The death of my grandmother.

It was the first time I saw my father cry. We all went to the funeral some fifty kilometres away. It was common practice to view the dead before burial. My brother and I watched her closely. When I tried to touch her face, my brother slapped me. Later on we laughed and joked about the way she looked. Then everybody started to drink and eat and have a party.

My father was sure that we were related to the painter Jan Vermeer. One day he took my brother and me to Nymegen, his birthplace, where we visited our great-great grandmother who was, according to my father, ninety-seven years old and definitely a Vermeer. Indeed, a small shingle read 'Cornelia Vermeer'. We climbed the narrow stairs and found an ancient woman with a remarkable little dog. The dog could perform some memorable tricks — balancing a plate on its nose, standing on one leg or walking on two, dancing, singing ... There was no limit to his genius. How could she not have been a Vermeer with a dog like that?

When I was about twelve, we moved into the city. My father had rented a three-storey house with a shop front, not far off the main street. The house stood forlorn in the ruins and the rubble that still hadn't been cleared up so many years after the war. An attempt was made to recreate the city in its original form. This house was the first, built in a most extraordinary shape which defies description. The cellars were full of water and already some of the new wallpaper was peeling off. Moisture ran off the walls. We thought we were in paradise. From the balcony at the back, we had an 180-degree view of the devastated city. Slowly other houses grew out of the rubble and slowly we became imprisoned in our paradise.

The first night in my new room didn't bring much sleep. Although the bridge was some distance away, we could hear the trains echoing through the empty wasteland in front of the house. That night I travelled by train through tunnels and bridges, across mountains and deserts. When I first read van Gogh's comment: 'Life is like a one-way journey on a train. You go so fast and cannot distinguish any object very clearly, and above all you never see the engine,' I relived every moment of that endless night.

But the house of my early youth will never be forgotten. I still remember every door, every room and all the corridors. Down to the colour of the wallpaper, the staircase, even the door handles. The worn steps to the endless cellars and the low windows that caught the evening sun. The warmth of that house has never been recaptured.

Some years ago I returned there. Casually strolled along the street and nervously stopped at Number 23. Went around the back to peep into the garden that had always loomed so large in my memory. Here was a patch of soil barely twenty by four metres, with no cherry tree. Where was the chicken pen? Where was the cave under the ground that we had built with the help of my uncle and where one could hide and sit in silence and pretend that the world outside did not exist? What had happened to that enormous garden of my youth? Why had it grown so small?

My idle thoughts were rudely interrupted by the arrival of the local police. They had received an urgent call to arrest this stranger 'staring at their garden'. It took me some time to convince the police that I was not a peeping Tom.

My uncle, who was born on the first of April, lived out of town in a strange house facing the forest. Hidden amongst the trees stood a German bunker, left in perfect condition. I don't understand now why we played violent war games around this bunker and why my uncle didn't stop us. Once I was badly wounded by 'enemy' fire and thrown into a ditch to die. I took my 'injuries' so seriously that when it was time to return home, I stubbornly refused to regain consciousness. My worried sisters and brother had to carry me back on a makeshift stretcher.

My uncle was a kind man, who always stood by to help us with broken toys or broken bicycles. He loved hunting and racing fast cars and motorbikes — sports I've learned to detest. But I admired my uncle and gladly accepted everything he did. On the back of his bike we once clocked 150 kilometres per hour. He begged me never to tell my parents.

One day he showed me how to load and fire a gun. In an apple tree nearby, a small bird was singing its heart out. I pulled the trigger; the bird fell to the ground. In great excitement, I rushed forward. The bird was still alive. I felt its warmth. My uncle said: 'You have to kill it. Throw it hard against the wall'. When I heard the thump of that bird against the grey stone, something died in me. The dryness of that sound — it had no echo. Then a last flutter, eyelids closed, a small spot of blood, a torn wing, a few small feathers dancing in the wind. The horror of it all became too much. I started to howl. I fully realised that I was losing my uncle's respect, but my agony and self pity were too great.

Apart from a fish I once caught by accident, I've never been able to hunt or fish and I still feel sickened by anything that reminds me of this dreadful event.

In the seventies my brother Wim and I crossed the Austrian border into Hungary. The train was searched by the Hungarian police. A bunch of hideous apes marched into our compartment and started to boss us around. Instinctively my brother and I drew close to each other. This sort of human behaviour we remembered from the war. We were searched and humiliated. An old man was arrested, a crying woman abused and taken away, a young boy beaten. Nobody dared protest, including us.

I had been living on the other side of the world for too long. This journey was part of the reawakening of an old friendship. A shy, brotherly friendship in which we were both desperately trying to make contact again. We needed to listen to one another. We needed to travel together — to become brothers again. Although almost forty, my brother had only just discovered that he, too, had an artistic soul that needed to blossom. A year before my departure for Australia he and his wife Yvonne had fled to Germany. His business as an industrial photographer was booming but the work he produced didn't match the poetry in his heart. Since that time he's held numerous photographic exhibitions and published several books.

I had a few films in my suitcase that, if discovered, could have put us both in jail. When they came to my luggage, I eagerly offered my assistance. 'Please make it short and take me away. Please put us both in a cell so that we can talk in peace and share our memories.' Secretly I prayed to be exposed, to be arrested. No such luck! My eagerness to co-operate threw the apes. My brother's luggage, however, was meticulously examined. He had nothing to hide yet died a thousand deaths. Fear of injustice is one of the worst fears.

In the midst of this pathetic display of human stupidity, a flock of birds flew across the border. They didn't need passports or excuses. No other birds were trying to rape their dignity. I thought of that little bird in the cherry tree, its final flutter, that terrible thump against the grey stone, those small, dancing feathers … Then I understood and felt for a moment, with the greatest, all-embracing clarity, the word 'freedom'. My brother and I started to talk, we touched in mid-air and were free.

The new house never felt right and my parents seemed to have lost one another in the process of moving. At school I tried hard to please, to show some intelligence; fluctuated between brilliance and utter stupidity, suffered unbearable shyness, tried to be part of the system and never quite made it. I wrote an essay about the sinking of the *Titanic*. The teacher was most impressed but didn't think it possible that I'd written this myself. Why didn't he trust me? I'd written about the yellow lights streaming out of portholes, about the band that went down whilst playing their instruments. I'd written about 'shadows being eaten by the waves' and the lifeless body of a child drifting in the ocean. The teacher found it all very odd. 'Eerie and a bit crazy'. How could this emerge from such an immature mind?

The next essay was about the coalminers in the south. I dug a deep hole under the ground, with twisted alleyways and dark chambers. I wrote about the blackened faces of the miners, the despair and poverty of their families. I described in the finest detail the atmosphere in the villages and the smoke that rose from chimneys obscuring the evening sun. This time the teacher was convinced of my potential, as the story was written during class. But then we were asked to write about politics and religion and immediately I lost my accumulated favour.

I don't think I learned very much at school. Everything that awakened in me was crushed. I felt different from my fellow students. I was alone. I felt handicapped. Even now when I glance at myself, I recognise that wearing the same black jacket every day is an expression of solitude, affirming my absence.

Wim and I leaving for Hungary.

All the children together after the birth of Christa, the youngest child.

When I was about fifteen, it suddenly occurred to me that I was going to die, that my mother was going to die, my father, my sisters, my brother. Behind every face there was a skull. During my whole life I've never been able to forget the total horror that struck me after this discovery. It seemed so useless to keep going — to keep going to school, to eat and sleep, to laugh and cry. Why live and love, only to be wasted in the end? This fact presented itself with such totality that a terrible sense of doom pervaded my being. I hid in the attic, unable to speak or move.

After a few days my worried mother took me for a walk. We walked for hours in the rain along the murky river, upon the cobblestones of my youth. At the edge of town, my desperate mother held me so tightly that it hurt. I wept and wept; she cried with me. We approached our house. In total desperation my mother said: 'When I was your age, I felt exactly the same.' Slowly that terrible feeling of doom and loneliness disappeared. We went inside; the rain had ceased.

Being in town helped to improve my father's photographic business. He couldn't relate very well to anyone outside of his narrow kingdom, but needed an assistant. When my eldest sister Elizabeth failed one of her exams, she was introduced into the photographic world and pressured into helping him. My father was a perfectionist, would spend hours retouching an obscure photograph or negative and displayed the same obsessive behaviour when he decided to clean the show windows or polish the tiled floor. He expected the same fastidiousness and eye for detail from all around.

In the living room stood an old cabinet in which my father stored a small safe and some boxes with his papers. No one was allowed to touch this cabinet or look inside, including my mother. After closing the shop, my father would come upstairs and put whatever he didn't want to leave downstairs into this strange piece of furniture. One of the greatest horrors of my youth was my father's daily black mass in front of this cabinet. A manic performance that we were forced to watch from a far corner of the room. My father would kneel down in the greatest concentration, often whisper to himself, then rattle a bunch of keys and select one at random. No one was allowed to discover which key he needed, so he played all sorts of tricks to fool us. Of course the first key wouldn't fit, which gave him reason enough to get upset and look around as if there were someone he could accuse of having stolen the important key. Then he would put the right key in the lock and pretend it didn't work. Had anyone fiddled with the lock? Finally the real job of opening the door would commence. The key would go in and out of the lock several times, before the first serious attempt was made to turn the key. Although we would pretend to be busy with homework or other matters, the tension all this created was enormous. Hearing the lock click didn't mean he would open the door straight away. Sometimes he would remove the key and start afresh.

The closing of the cabinet was an even bigger and more complicated task. To check whether the door was really locked, he would open it again and consequently have to repeat the earlier routine. When finally satisfied he would pull the door with his fingers and put his ear against it. What he listened to remains a mystery. This totally lunatic behaviour left us in a state of hypnotic terror.

I won't go into details about what was required to turn off the gas. This was beyond description. Once we were all gathered to go on a rare Sunday afternoon stroll, but only made it to the front door. My father needed an hour and a half to perform his duties after which we were all too exhausted to go outside. This extreme behaviour peaked when I was about seventeen. It was fascinating and frightening. If my mother made any comment at all, he would fly into a rage and accuse her and her children of the most ridiculous conspiracies. You might think that these recollections are exaggerated. I wish this were true.

The worst day of my early youth was Christmas 1952. An extra large Christmas tree stood in one corner. New coloured lights were flashing in all directions. My mother had set the dinner table with fine old china and silverware from her past, and little candles in front of each plate.

Outside it was grey and cold. A thin blanket of snow covered the roofs of our town. Inside, the warmth and cosiness of a family Christmas. Silent night, holy night. Peace on earth to all people of goodwill. We felt very blessed and secure. Even my father seemed at peace. I felt happy; this was a rare moment of celebration. In church the pastor had told us to love everyone and everything, to forgive, to embrace. Yes, I did love everyone and everything. I loved my father, too. Of course I loved him. It surprised me that, for the very first time, I felt true compassion for him. If only I could find a way to show this.

Through the silences and the clicking of forks and spoons, a tension began to build. Something was amiss. We all knew that my father couldn't bear Sundays or holidays — but surely this Christmas was special. Nothing could touch the fire of this spirit. This was the start of a new beginning. Everything lay ahead.

From across the street accordion music could be heard and the voices of children singing. It was a touching sound of unity and togetherness. It moved us. My father thought they were making too much noise, but my mother said gently, 'They are celebrating ... they are happy.' The next moment our merry Christmas was ruined forever. My father angrily banged his fist on the table and yanked the tablecloth. In one violent action my mother's precious china flew everywhere and our peaceful dreams were shattered forever. A devastating awakening to our reality.

My father's angry gesture caused an enormous hurt in all of us. There hasn't been one Christmas since that fateful day, when I haven't felt the same devastation. I still don't trust the Christmas spirit — barely managing to get through those days — and feel enormous relief when Christmas is over and all the jingle bells have been silenced once again.

After Elizabeth had been initiated, my father set her up in the damp cellars of the building. Her own dark room, her own kingdom. She was seventeen, tender and shy. Alone. I'm recalling all this with a degree of irony, but that's not how I felt at the time. I looked up to her. She had my father's respect, or so it seemed. Of course my father meant well, but he was a wounded artist. He'd once seen and experienced the larger picture but was too devastated by what happened during the war to climb the mountain again. It had confirmed the dark side of his heart and he stuck to it, forcing everybody around him to suffer the same fate. Dear Elizabeth. She was hardly allowed out of the house but spent ten years printing little photographs for my father's customers. I think she was twenty-five before she ever went out with a man. A prisoner in her cave, dutiful and meticulous, silently losing her youth.

My second sister, Jacoba, was a little more fortunate. She managed well at school and went on to become a teacher. She could draw and paint and often left little poems under my pillow at night. I admired her. Both sisters suffered much fear and frustration. For some reason they were allowed to join a local ballet company, where they could escape twice a week. We never got to know one another very well. I feel their depth and their love, but the real human complexity between us has few words. With my brother and two younger sisters there's a different, more humorous bond that became stronger after we separated and makes it easier to reconnect each time we meet. My brother and I now work together on books and exhibitions. My younger sister, Angeline, a fine artist in her own right, gives me much support and faith, and my younger sister, Christa, offers light and humour in moments of despair.

When my brother finished his secondary education, he was also recruited by my father and when business was booming I, too, had to spend all my spare time as a dark-room assistant.

The whole family now worked together, with my father despotically running the shop. A few relics of his past found their

Jacoba and Elizabeth.

way to the attic — an old projector, some winders, empty cans, rolls of film, mysterious objects that fascinated me. Two windows looked out onto the sky. In summer, the sun would slowly travel through the attic. I could sit there for hours, watching the light come and go. Now and then my mother would climb the stairs and sit with me. We shared many secrets and much unhappiness. During the slow decay of my childhood, she was the only person who could soothe the pain of that deathly loneliness.

At nineteen I was conscripted to join the army. It came as some relief. I thought this would liberate me from the prison I had grown up in and in my ignorance I set off enthusiastically. Dear me, what a shock to my fragile system. It still took a few days to realise that there was something drastically wrong here. Who were these people who saluted one another in passing, marched like ducks doing the rounds, practised ridiculous useless skills like killing people? What was the purpose of all this?

Because my bed wasn't made properly (I'd turned the top sheet once instead of twice), I was marched off, together with a small group of unfortunates, to help the kitchen staff clean dirty pots and pans. Everything had to be absolutely spotless and an eager young corporal was given the important job of keeping an eye on us. Every time I finished a pot, he would inspect it meticulously and return it. Not good enough: 'Where do you come from? You think you're too good for this, don't you?'. Well into the afternoon I still hadn't produced one clean pot that could pass his skilful eye. I'd already been treated, or rather ridiculed, by an army psychiatrist for severe depression and was in the lowest spirits possible. I finally stood up and politely asked for permission to go to the toilet. 'Not until you've produced at least one clean pot that can pass.' A dormant anger that had slowly been developing, matured in one split second. I flew across the kitchen, grabbed the poor man by his neck and bashed his head against the largest pot in sight. He was bigger and certainly more athletic than I, but against my anger he didn't stand a chance. The cook and his staff came to his rescue and of course reported the incident. A sympathetic captain, who somehow understood and felt my despair, saved me from a long prison sentence. To match anger with physical aggression is pretty appalling. Lest we forget ...

An accident put an end to my misfortunes. I played hockey on my free weekends. Someone from the opposing team missed the ball and hit me hard in the knee, which blew up like a balloon. In the army hospital some clumsy trainee stuck a long thick needle into my leg to suck out the fluid; the needle struck something delicate and caused an even bigger haemorrhage. After a while the army dispatched me to a rehabilitation centre where I spent many months recuperating, playing volleyball, sitting on the floor reading books and studying the ingenuity of modern warfare. When I started to walk without a limp — I kept it up as long as possible — I was returned to the troops and together with another misplaced soldier, Harry Benders, finished up as a coffee and tea maker for the officers.

Harry introduced me to the art of reading. We read every classic, every book of interest, from Kierkegaard to Sartre, from André Gide's *L'Immoraliste* to Albert Camus' *L'Etranger*. Franz Kafka's *The Castle* impressed me so much that I read it three times. It was a profound initiation. These were inspiring stories that brought a vivid imagery to my mind. It seemed that my real education had only just begun. The army finally discharged me.

I enrolled at an art school but my father opposed this very strongly. How could I let my mother down and leave the house? My mother helped me and kept silent. So I attended art school at night, in secret. It wasn't so much that I wanted to study art or become a so-called artist; I needed to find a peer group, to relate to people of like mind, people with similar interests and obsessions.

Then my father allowed me to do a correspondence course in photography, which took me to the big city once a month.

Meanwhile he taught me the art of photography in the most medieval way. In retrospect, I'm thankful for this.

At twenty-one — or was it nineteen? — I travelled to Paris with my mother. This was a dramatic turning point in my life. A neighbour took us in his car. As soon as we hit the outskirts of our town, a heavy mist came down and within minutes we had an accident. Nobody was injured, but the car was badly damaged. When I heard the driver say: 'We'd better give it a rest ... stay at home', I was so deeply frustrated that for the first time in my life, I raised my voice and pleaded with him and my mother to get another car, to continue the journey. Everyone was surprised, especially my mother, with my pleas. But they did respond, got another vehicle and we arrived in Paris with no further incident. It was crucial for me to make this journey. I would have walked. I knew that this was terribly important.

My mother and I walked the streets of Paris; we went to the Louvre, sat in cafes, had long animated dinners with her family. I had managed to extract an old camera from my father's shop. It took six photographs on a roll of twelve and would jam at the most crucial moments. This was the best camera my father could lend me. In that one week my horizon changed. I suddenly grew up, realised that deep down I was an adventurer by nature. This city was breathing, I could feel its heart. It was the beginning of a journey. Despite the broken camera, the photographs I brought back are still the best I ever took.

One photograph stands out in particular. A little girl sitting on a chair, dreamily watching the world. She'd probably spotted me, but wasn't interested. She was simply satisfied with her view. Her distant gaze embraced the whole of Paris and beyond. I knelt down, waited for a couple to walk past in the background to balance the picture. Miraculously, the camera worked. I'd consciously composed an image that reflected my deepest thoughts and feelings. My mother, who'd waited patiently, said: 'That will be a beautiful photograph'.

In a Paris park, c.1958.

Leaving home.

Leaving Home

The Australian Government had launched a post-war immigration program and was offering young people — students and professionals — a chance to live in Australia for six months to a year with the purpose of promoting Australia on their return. I saw this advertised in the paper and, in great secrecy, applied. I simply had to get away from my family as far as possible, and here was a chance to escape. I needed to find a way to open up, to unlock that iron door inside, to be alone from family influence and pain. To save myself.

My mother knew that I had been accepted, but we didn't dare tell my father. When he did learn of it a few days before my departure, he did his utmost to stop me. But I was determined and went. Left my mother in a flood of tears and watched my lonely father, cold and grey, staring helplessly away from me beside the train.

I wept all the way down to the west of Holland, on the boat crossing the Channel, on the train to Southampton. I was a very protected, backward little boy — not fit for human consumption. My mother had sewn zippers into all my pockets because she thought I would get robbed. I was twenty-two years old. I came from a different century.

It's hard to describe the cleansing of emotions I experienced travelling across the ocean on an old Italian liner to Australia, despite the fact that Holland was my birthplace. I had never seen the sea. The sea was more immense to me than the universe. What longing, what loneliness in that vastness, in that endless waterland. I kept drowning and awakening. Drifted for miles and miles into the unknown. The sea was travelling with me; I felt safe.

After a few weeks, however, I started to imagine that I'd fallen overboard and was drifting in the ocean — totally lost, totally alone, totally doomed. Overriding all this, I felt a mad passion to embrace — to embrace the world as large as it is. Now I know that that total embrace is also the final embrace.

Then I met an English girl called Tina. She was quiet and thoughtful and lovely to look at. I was far too shy to confront her, so I watched her in secret until one night the gods kindly seated me next to her. She reminded me of Marlies, the girl I'd loved and adored in Holland, with whom I had performed all types of acrobatics except intercourse. In our Catholic world, love-making was against God, Queen and country.

That night, the white flickering light of my youth was extinguished.

In Port Said I bought a cheap transistor radio and for the first time in my life, listened to the world. Yes, the whole world passed through my hands at the slightest touch of the dial. The music and voices were so unfamiliar, yet made me feel totally at home. What a world out there. What colour, what excitement! And all this from a transistor, tax free.

Tina ignored me for the rest of the journey, which I could not understand. I performed all types of tricks to draw her attention. Even joined the sun worshippers on deck to cultivate a quick tan, but woke up in the soothing wind with a strange burning feeling in my chest. A few hours later, large blisters popped up through the red skin and the next weeks were spent in agony lying on my bed.

A similar thing had happened to me once before when I tried to impress a girl in the local swimming pool at home. I had forced my mother to buy me a cheap pair of leopard-skin bathers that would make me look nonchalantly masculine. When I emerged from the changing cubicle it slowly dawned on me that I looked ridiculous. What could I do but start running? I would run so fast that nobody could focus on me. Alas, tragedy struck. I ran full blast into an iron pole and had to be carried off on a stretcher.

As we were approaching Australia, a wild storm shook the boat. In the lounge a prim English lady vomited down her husband's neck; an elderly couple who had struggled along ropes for half an hour to get to the other side of the dance floor found themselves back where they started in three seconds flat. The tragi-comic nature of the human race presented itself with great fragility. One never knew whether to laugh or cry. The safest was to do both.

I was strangely moved when we spotted Fremantle. Too many weeks at sea makes the heart melt. Australia looked large and ancient. We took a rattling train to Perth and walked the streets in the greatest delight. It was a beautiful city with the most wonderful buildings and streets. Perth has now almost caught up with the rest of the world. A miniature New York looms from the desert. Most historic buildings have been destroyed and replaced with concrete blocks with no past and no future. On a recent visit I saw a beautiful old building advertised as a 'Splendid Development Site'. Meanwhile Perth prides itself on having more millionaires per square kilometre than anywhere else in the world.

In Melbourne I was put ashore. I had wanted to go to Sydney, but fate decided otherwise. My first months in Australia were absolutely terrible; I walked the deserted streets in the greatest despair. Where was the village square? Where were the people? What sort of life was this?

I had no money and no home. Had nothing in common with the people in the hostel I was buried in. And on top of this I didn't understand their language. The Australian slang sounded crude and impossible to comprehend, and my English wasn't very good either.

My first job was as a camera salesman in a suburban photographic store. Over the weekends I worked for a place called Social Snaps, which took me into ballrooms, schools and wedding parties. At one of the school parties I met a sweet girl called Suzie but her parents didn't want her to go out with a foreigner — especially not with one who wore sandals. So we met in secret. I read her German poetry, for which she had a passion, and took her for walks along the river. We've always stayed in touch. The Social Snaps owner forced me to buy a dinner suit to impress his customers. I found one in an opportunity shop for the mighty price of two pounds. The trousers were so large that I had to strap them under my arms. When we went into the dance halls a large Hungarian was my mentor. He was obsessed with sex and often managed to seduce — quite literally — the girls right under the eyes of their boyfriends.

With my friend Jan from the boat I finally moved into a 'flatette' where we listened to music. Jan was hooked on classical music and played the same old records on his old gramophone. He really loved Beethoven, which seemed rather odd to me. Classical music was part of my upbringing and the worshipping of something I knew so well puzzled me.

Not that we had had an extensive library of classical records at home, but the classical radio hour and the 'opera hour' we never missed. Even at that stage I found music very comforting and, although I knew how to hum a few popular tunes, I was extremely selective. In a cupboard next to the old black and white television was a record collection of maybe forty records. A large 78 recording of Saint-Saens's *Samson and Delilah*. Small LP's of Sibelius' *Valse Triste* and *Finlandia* and, of course, *Eine Kleine Nachtmusik*. Due to my two older sisters' passionate involvement with the local ballet company we had *Der Fledermaus, Swan Lake* and some Franz Lehar music. The lyrics, sung in German, still haunt me like the plague. When there was nobody at home I played Beethoven. This was slightly unusual for a ten or twelve-year-old. and I was afraid of being laughed at. So I made sure I was alone and then played Beethoven as loudly as possible. I think it was Anthony Burgess who said: 'After Mozart, all music stopped'. Of course this is a dreadful exaggeration, but ...

The twentieth century gave us the means to communicate, but with it came the noise of our time, the greed of our time ... or rather, the noise of our greed. Mozart knew the force of silence. We can always return to him. Find solace and new hope. The thought that mankind might cease to exist one day is extremely disturbing and the thought that there would be no music, no Mozart, no Beethoven, no Vincent van Gogh, no Nijinsky, no Tagore, is too miserable to contemplate.

Somehow Jan's obsession confirmed my traditional closeness to classical music and I became a devout classical groupie. When I left Australia the first time I travelled with little else than stacks of classical records. They were my companions in difficult times. Music is the basis of all creativity and as W.B. Yeats said: 'Everybody's life is a symphony.'

In Spain recently, I joined a group of people for dinner at a Basque restaurant. The owner apologised for the piped muzak and said: 'This is what people want ... not my choice.' 'A Basque restaurant should have Basque music,' I suggested meekly. He started to sing an old song from the old mountains with an old voice that came straight from the soil of Spain. Two Basque women instantly burst into tears. The others, mesmerised and overcome. Pain and joy had the same face. I don't think anyone present will ever forget that evening. We had all received the great gift of true passion and our spirits soared. They soared because of music.

Before every film, I usually have the music in place. It helps greatly with the actual making of the film. The picture is composed to the music and never the other way around. Music has much more to do with film than literature or the theatre. Music, dance, painting — in that order — are more related to film than theatre or literature.

The owner of Social Snaps decided that, in the end, I wasn't social enough, reimbursed me for the dinner suit and sent me packing. As a camera salesman I was more successful, but the job wasn't very satisfying.

I enrolled at Melbourne University and then fell madly in love. I say 'madly' because all those months of isolation had created a certain imbalance in my system. Poor Carol. I don't think she ever really understood my crazy love for her. It must have been dreadful to be haunted by this maniac, who had no ability at all to express his passion. I loved her desperately and wanted to marry her. Fortunately, she stopped me. Twenty-six years later I met her again at a school fete; she with her two sons, me with my daughter. At first I didn't recognise her. A mature, middle-aged woman; wrinkles, greyness through her red hair. Then she smiled and suddenly I plunged back through time and space and remembered ...

After eighteen months I left Australia with more despair in my heart than ever before. What to do now? Where to go? Found a place on a French cargo boat together with a small group of travellers and spent many months drifting back to Europe. It was an adventurous trip with brawls and booze, with prostitutes in foreign ports. I started to realise that the world was not what I had imagined or expected it to be. This was a rough place, full of violence and injustice — but I was living.

The line 'prostitutes in foreign ports' was questioned by a friend: 'You never told me.' I should have said that I *watched* prostitutes in foreign ports. One has to be so careful. But it led to the following recollection.

In Martinique I went for a walk with one of the ship's cooks. We found a small cafe run by a very beautiful young girl. She was friendly and warm, with a great sense of fun. We drank one rum and coke after the other, half of them with compliments from the management. The girl kept filling our glasses, then invited me into the back room. I thought she wanted to show me her etchings, but she slipped off her dress and said, 'First time is free.' My mother had warned me that 'one moment of pleasure can cause a lifetime of grief'. The girl misunderstood my hesitation, thought that she wasn't clean enough and asked her grandmother to give her a bath. They took me into a backyard full of chickens and a large pig. The grandmother started to hose the girl off and sponge her with soap. They were laughing and making fun of me. Then the grandmother stole my sandals and would only return them if I made love to her granddaughter. I'd never encountered such totally uninhibited people and asked for more drinks to put me at ease. The girl was disappointed and wanted to teach me a lesson. The cook was taken into the back room and I could come and watch or wait my turn.

I left my sandals and struggled back to the boat. The cook returned late at night with some amazing stories, and thought I was the biggest fool around. I, too, regretted my cowardice and would have gone back next day if the boat hadn't sailed in the morning. By the time we reached Marseilles, the cook had a solid dose of gonorrhoea and cursed the hell out of me.

The night before my departure was spent in Sydney with Sue, a friend of Carol's. She had played Rachmaninoff's Second Piano Concerto daily for many years. I understood her. We stayed at her uncle's place and sat the whole night on the balcony watching the old couple play alcoholic games. The next day she came to the wharf. It was a lonely, painful farewell. The world seemed so large and cruel around us. We weren't lovers, just two highly sensitive souls who felt united through a mutual friend, sharing an intimate smallness that has grown very large throughout the years.

She never moved as the boat sailed. Her tiny figure, forlorn on the shore. The salt of her tears on my cheeks. The look of total despair in her eyes. The further I sailed away, the stronger our human bond became. Now I see her very rarely, once a year, maybe once every two years. But there is always the same softness, the same mysterious connection. Only in growing older do we see how rare this beauty is. How human bonds can grow beyond friendship, beyond physical closeness. Through age we see how miraculous it is that flowers bloom in the midst of ruins. How poetry survives in the midst of oppression. There is another world and it is in this one. It's not outside, it's inside, wholly inside.

The cargo boat docked at the most exotic and fascinating places. Lost little islands in the Pacific where people welcomed us as liberators. When the cargo was loaded or off-loaded, I had days to walk around the islands with my camera. Bernard Shaw once said that photographers were like codfish that lay a million eggs in order to hatch one. I had a very limited supply of film, I couldn't afford to take many photographs and thus every picture became an event of sorts.

Once I walked past two young girls, standing in the rain with wise old smiles and tender eyes full of hope. They reminded me of that little girl in Paris, even though they looked directly at me. There was that same distant connection with the beyond. 'Mind and reason

I often look at this image. It connects me with 'reality'.

instinctively freed from all mortality.' They didn't move as I took one simple, direct photograph. I often look at this image. It connects me with 'reality'.

Back in Holland I held two photographic exhibitions. The modest success I enjoyed with these shows gave me some hope, some direction. I must thank the Dutch art critic Willem Coumans for this, who saw more in my photographs than I did at the time. After six months or so I had to return to Australia. The image of Carol kept haunting me. I also felt that I had lost Europe forever. I had never read much about the East, but I had strange dreams at night and a great longing to see more of the world. Again I departed in great pain, leaving my dear mother shattered, and even kissed my father before boarding the plane. Carol was still there, loving me on the one hand and struggling to find her own identity. When finally she started to love me that soft singing of my blood for her ceased.

I had saved enough money to buy a small motor car. Within a few weeks I had a bad accident, driving back from the country. The girl I was with had fallen asleep on my lap and after a while I, too, dozed off. When I woke up the car had more or less disintegrated around us. My first impulse was to push the accelerator. I couldn't understand why we weren't moving. Then I saw her bleeding face in front of the car. She was crying and calling out. I had great difficulty breathing, could feel my life ebbing away. A meadow of my youth opened up ... a face in the mist ... a single crow. Bare, knotted willow trees near water. The face of my mother. I was sinking into the deep. Apart from the bitter-sweet taste of blood in my mouth, it was quite a pleasant experience. From the corner of my eye I saw the tattooed arm of a tow-truck man. A piece of paper was put in front of me. A heavy voice: 'Sign this, mate.' My surrender to those white wings of death was rudely interrupted. I'm sure to this day that the sudden fury that made my body shake, saved my life. How could I possibly die in front of this ghoul? The poor man had brought me back to life. I knew I would live.

A few weeks later, when I came out of hospital, the man sent me a cheque for eight pounds, the value of the tyres. The cheque bounced.

I was twenty-five when I started a little photographic studio. I photographed weddings, mothers with their babies, lovers, old and young. Anyone or anything that seemed of interest. A young poet asked me to take his portrait, a sensitive young man with large blue eyes. He recited his poems as I photographed him. Romantic poems about loneliness and despair, sorrow and tenderness, about the terrible spirit of death. We went into the park across the road and I photographed him walking towards me with a receding row of bare trees behind him. He was going on a journey and would contact me on his return. A week later Brian Heath, a local minister, came to see me. The young poet had killed himself.

My studio consisted of a front room, a show window and a back room for a darkroom, sleeping and eating. The toilet was in the backyard, which I shared with the people upstairs. With my friend Bernie Eddy I made silly little films on Super 8. We made 'The Drowning of W.C. Fields' (I played the lead; the climax came when I walked into the ocean wearing flippers and an old dinner jacket), 'The Woman Who Couldn't Say No' and 'Why Fish Need Water'. Fortunately these 'amazing' creations have been lost. The people upstairs moved out. My empire expanded. The darkroom went upstairs, the studio was enlarged and I bought a real bed. Somehow I'd found a road to travel on and, despite the regular depressions, a direction to follow. With the help of Joan Healey and Marianne Baillieu I staged a few photographic exhibitions which helped me grow more confident and more at home.

After the initial burst of silly shorts, Bernie and I tried something bigger, something with a bit more substance. He was the organiser and the front man, extroverted and outrageous. I was a helpless introvert, brooding and shy. I enjoyed his company enormously.

Bernie's lack of punctuality introduced me to Nijinsky, the great Russian dancer. One day I arrived to collect Bernie for a trip, but I found him still recovering from a night on the town. As I waited impatiently for him to emerge, my attention was drawn to a voice coming from an adjoining room — Paul Scofield reading from Nijinsky's notebooks on the radio. 'I'm not an ordinary man ... I am a dancer ... You will understand me when you see me dance ...'

That was my introduction to the magic of Nijinsky. 'You will understand me when you see me dance', hit me with great force. Yes, why was language the only way of communication? Why did everything need to be explained through speech? Film had only just begun to fascinate me. I could 'smell' its potential but had great trouble using words to explain what I was trying to say.

I heard more that afternoon. 'I'm a man in a million ... I'm a dancer. I'm a madman who loves mankind. My madness is my love for mankind ...'

A few weeks later I went to London, searched the bookshops and found a little book called *The Diary of Vaslav Nijinsky*, edited by Romola Nijinsky, his wife. I read the diary that afternoon, sitting in my cheap hotel room. Close by, a church bell would strike every half hour. Stray pigeons would land on the window sill and warm themselves in the pale sunlight. I heard the bell, saw the pigeons but nothing really registered. When I put the book down, I sat quietly in the fading light and wept. I phoned my mother: 'Have you ever heard of Nijinsky?'. 'Yes, he was a great dancer. I had a

Vaslav Nijinsky. 'You will understand me when you see me dance'.

picture of him on my bedroom wall ... lost it somehow when I moved to Holland.' 'I've just read his notebooks. They're very beautiful. Wish I could find you a copy in French or German, or Dutch.' My mother simply said: 'Tell me about him when you come ... come soon.'

This happened some twenty-five years ago. In that time I have made fourteen feature films, many shorts, films for children and documentaries. During all that time, Nijinsky has travelled with me. When I was promoting *Vincent, the Life and Death of Vincent van Gogh* in the United States, I often drew a parallel between van Gogh's letters and Nijinsky's writings. Both were seekers of that white light — both wanted nothing but the truth. One of the interviews was heard or seen by Tamara, Nijinsky's second daughter, who wrote me a letter. We started to correspond, which led to an option to base a film on the notebooks but, more importantly, to a wonderful friendship that has embraced Tamara's daughter, Kinga, and the rest of the family.

Our children grow up with the wrong gods — people with little substance who are celebrated out of all proportion. We're so helpless in the face of this shallowness, so misguided. How can anyone find substance in life when all we hear and see is only skin deep? The great sixteenth-century poet, François Villon, wrote, 'It's your own fault, dear fellow citizen, that my life blossoms more beautifully than yours.' Nijinsky is one of the great romantic heroes of this century. He changed 'the dance' forever, invented a new form.

The Hindu have a practice of generating a force that counteracts gravitation. They say that he who awakens the *anahata chakra* — situated in the heart and the seat of all cosmic energy — can walk in the air. Nijinsky had the ability to remain suspended in the air at the highest point of elevation, before descending. 'That high note, sustained — taken — and held to the end.' But Nijinsky was much more than the god of the dance; he was a humanitarian, a seeker of truth. In the preface to his *Diary*, Romola Nijinsky wrote:

> Nijinsky devoted all his life, his soul, his genius, to the service of humanity, with the intention of ennobling and uplifting his audience to bring art, beauty and joy to the world. His aim was not to entertain or to reap success and glory for himself, but to transmit a divine message through his own medium — the dance. He could not escape, with his incorporeal, sensitive nature, the fate of all great humanitarians, to be sacrificed.

Nijinsky himself wrote:

> Once in the mountains I came to a road which led to a peak. I climbed up and stopped. I wanted to make a speech on the mountain; I had the desire to do so. I felt no pain, but a great love towards people. I wanted to jump from the top of the mountain into the village of St. Moritz. I did not because I had to go further. I went on and came to a tree. The tree told me that one could not speak here, because human beings do not understand feeling. I went on. I was sorry to part with the tree, because the tree understood me. I walked. I climbed up to the altitude of two thousand metres — stood there a long time. I felt a voice and shouted in French: '*Parole!*'. I wanted to speak, but my voice was so strong that I could only shout: 'I love everyone! I want happiness! I love everyone! I want everyone!.

Yes, that moment of total elation — all-embracing, accepting, forgiving. Only in the last few years have I come to realise how much of Nijinsky's spirit has penetrated my heart, and thus found a way into my films.

The Australian Ballet commissioned me to do a promotional booklet, which I accepted with great enthusiasm. To watch the dance close by, to capture that moment of elation, was a wonderful challenge. It led to me becoming the still photographer on the set of *Don Quixote*, directed and produced by Robert Helpmann and Rudolf Nureyev. It was my first experience of a large production. The wastage and intrigue was fascinating. Here I met Tibor Markus, a Hungarian actor, filmmaker and art director, who later produced my first feature, *Illuminations*. In *Don Quixote*, Tibor was the man in charge of props. When Robert Helpmann's horse died on the set, Tibor was given the delicate task of replacing the dead beast with a live one — or at least a horse that could stand on its feet. Tibor went to the abattoir to find a replacement. He finally found a horse with a passing resemblance and sprayed the poor animal he had saved from the gallows in the same grey tones. Nobody noticed the difference.

I did not enjoy hanging around the set as a photographer and after a week I no longer had to worry. One day I photographed Nureyev during a rehearsal that didn't go very well and Rudy took it out on me; he flew past the camera and punched me hard on the nose. I'd upset him enough to be removed from the production. I was appalled by his rudeness. He treated the dancers with the same disdain and arrogance. I've never forgiven myself for not having returned a solid punch or two.

Each time I saved up some money, I would travel. Mostly to Indonesia and India. In fact, all the money I earned went on travel and on my hobby — making films.

I also went to New Guinea. A romantic journey in search of man's childhood. I tried to photograph a way of life that was rapidly vanishing from the earth. In the Highlands the people staged a sing

... *human sculptures, frozen in time.*

sing. Strange, stone-aged figures emerged from the low hanging mist. They formed a long line on a hill, stood there, silently, for some time. Then the first man produced an ancient howl and the others followed. If was as if a strong wind swept through the line like a fire, carrying me off into the forest and across the mountains. Later I found a few men in a dark hut, standing like statues carved out of black wood. I put my camera on a window sill and exposed for approximately five seconds, not expecting success. But when the image appeared later in my darkroom, I realised that they'd stood perfectly still, human sculptures, frozen in time. On my second visit to New Guinea, I met Ulli and Georgina Beier. Together we produced a book, *Home of Man — the people of New Guinea*. Ulli and his wife had already written, illustrated and edited many books on African art and artists, and Ulli had collected some intensely personal poetry written by his students at the university of Papua-New Guinea. My photographs try to complement these beautiful poems. We've remained close throughout the years and keep searching for the same truths.

One day a little lady walked into my studio. She had been attracted by the photographs I had on show in a city gallery and had come to 'meet the artist'. She then insisted that I come with her to look at her paintings and sculpture. I was a little taken aback and reluctantly closed shop. On the way to her home she told me that she was eighty-six and had just walked from the city to pay me a surprise visit. Even though she might have known a short cut through the parks, it still must have been at least six kilometres. After I had admired her paintings, she asked me whether I thought she had any future as a painter, or did I think she should concentrate more on sculpture?

Dear Ethel Barnes. She was an extraordinary, courageous and

Ethel Barnes.

gifted artist. A marvellous friend and soul mate with an insatiable passion for the arts. She was ageless and timeless and was of great importance to me in my transformation from photographer to filmmaker. We often went to see a film or visit the theatre. Mart Crowley's *The Boys in the Band* was her first confrontation with the 'theatre of four-letter words', as she called it. She was not impressed. 'It's not because they swear on stage — but these characters are so poor of heart and spirit. There's no joy, no humour.' She was glad to get back to her little house, which was called, 'My little womb'.

Once we went to the ballet and for over three hours watched Nureyev leap about. Ethel hadn't moved, not even at interval, and had grown rather stiff. As she got up she lost her balance and I just caught her before she hit the floor. 'I'm too old for a *pas de deux*,' she screamed in my ear. I spun around with her, pretending to do a pirouette, and Ethel's feet hit a rather sophisticated lady in the back. The woman looked at us with such disdain that Ethel burst into a loud chuckle. She became quite hysterical with laughter and couldn't stand up. I carried this screaming old lady past stunned ballet-lovers, down the stairs, through the foyer and into the street, where she finally calmed down.

At 103 she flew to the United States to spend the last few years of her life with her daughter. She was the oldest person ever to cross the Pacific by air. A local newspaper had dispatched a photographer. When he knelt down to take a photograph, Ethel said: 'Are you proposing, young man?'. On the eve of her departure, when we knew this was forever, she whispered in my ear: 'Don't ever let me down'.

Around the same time I'd met an actress called Sheila Florance, who stunned the local theatre patrons with her intense portrayal of middle-aged women. Sheila knew she had greatness. At the end of her life, when she was dying of cancer, we finally found a vehicle to express her wonderful lust for life. *A Woman's Tale* is the one film

I'm pleased with. It belongs to Sheila and to Ethel Barnes and to Jean Campbell, to Myrtle Woods, to Lady Viola Tait, Elsa Davies, Elena Leiss, Maria De-Marchi ... to all those great souls who cannot and will not give in, who keep living and giving and are never afraid of their age or impending death. A good film is a bit like that. A film that matters lives on, bypasses instant praise or rewards. A good film penetrates the psyche and thus lives and lingers forever.

I saw Serge Paradjanov's *Shadows of our Forgotten Ancestors* well before I started making films. It totally stunned me and left a big, bleeding hole inside. Throughout the years that wound became a treasure — a rich source of inspiration. Paradjanov wrote about these flashes of brilliance and of his aspiration to create a sustained work. 'That one high note, taken and held to the end.' Vincent van Gogh and Nijinsky spoke the same language. In his last letter, Paradjanov said: 'It's not an object in a story or in a photograph gives birth to a colour. It's the music of the object and the strangeness of the inner, lyrical, epic and dramatic reverberations of the story.' In *Shadows of our Forgotten Ancestors* he shows a man being struck with an axe. Blood pours over the screen and the next sequence is totally in red. I've never forgotten the music of this image. When Paradjanov was asked what concerned him in his films, he simply stated: 'Lust for life and nostalgia — what else is there?' When he was asked: 'How does it feel to have become a star?' he replied:

> What type of star? What do you mean? Stars are in the sky. How can you be a star at 63? I spent fifteen years in jail without underwear; the lice and fleas ate me alive. I'm an old man, sick and dying. I wake up in the morning screaming with pain. People run away from me in fright. What are you talking about, me a star! I've never heard such absurdity.

A local art school needed a part-time teacher to join their new photographic department. Some students had seen my photographs in the show window and asked me to apply. What started as a joke became a serious profession, although later on I realised that teaching cannot be a full-time profession. The teacher and the student must both be constantly involved in the process of learning, which becomes impossible on a full-time basis. Also, the people who make a profession out of teaching are often too caught up in their small political struggles and academic confusions to be able to give and receive freely. I was lucky. I knew nothing about teaching and therefore learned a lot doing it.

The art school was headed by a fine sculptor, Lenton Parr. A free thinker and visionary. He'd invited many artists to join his Australian 'Bauhaus' called Prahran College. Until the authorities closed in on him, this college had a significant impact on the development of the arts in Australia. I was joined by my friend and mentor, Athol Shmith, and later by John Cato, who will one day be recognised as one of the true greats in the art of photography.

When the faculty expanded and a lecturer in cinematography was needed, the job was mine. Apart from the few Super-8 movies I had made and some more serious attempts on 16mm, I knew nothing about filmmaking. I was forced to stay one step ahead of the students. That's how I became a filmmaker.

A New Beginning

If you want to do anything seriously, do it as a hobby. I've always believed this. As soon as it becomes your profession, a degree of compromise comes in. Vincent van Gogh says, 'How does one become mediocre? By compromising and making concessions, today in this matter, tomorrow in another, according to the dictates of the world, by never contradicting the world and by always following public opinion.'

Photography was my profession; cinematography my hobby. It was a safe start. My instinct has always rejected compromise and here my steady income protected me. But maybe the compromise was having a steady job.

The few films I went to see at this stage of my life puzzled me. What a lot of terrible rubbish was dished up to people! Stories larger than life with heroes larger than life embarrassed me. Violence — and especially violation of the spirit — confused me and, later on, angered me. I wanted to see real people. Real people were always larger than life to me. But what is reality? The way I went about making my films was already unreal enough.

Strangely enough, all my early films are quite surreal. In fact it would be better to call them 'unreal'. In the making of each picture, however, everything was totally clear to me, everything could be explained, everything was dripping with meaning. But as soon as a character developed too much for my liking, he or she had to disappear so that I could get on with my movie. I was totally blind to the possibility of revealing true emotions through actors. It was only when I discovered that after each film I could not remember what the meaning of it all was, that I realised something was drastically amiss. The only thing that was clear to me was the fact that through film I could explore the remote horizons of my dreams. Dreams would become reality in the absolute. That vast emptiness that surrounded and threatened me became habitable. But how to use film and communicate with others through film, without getting lost in distractions? How could I find — over and beyond appearances and beyond the mechanism of the movie making process — a truer reality? And how to avoid 'magnificent clarity' so that something remained a little later?

My first production, *Matuta*, a twenty-minute film on 16mm, almost cost me my life. We intended to start shooting at 5am and as we were all far too excited to sleep, spent the night drinking and working out shots. On the way to the set a car suddenly appeared from the side, travelling at high speed. I still don't know what made me turn the wheel. The car missed us by a fraction and flew off into the dark. I directed my first movie in an extremely confused state of mind. It shows.

Sometimes it is ignorance that helps us to push beyond common borders. The making of *The Journey* led to many discoveries that re-emerged later in my films. For eighteen months we filmed every weekend and waited anxiously during the rest of the week for the exposed film to return from the laboratory. 16mm diapositive needed to be sent to Kodak, who usually took their time. The original was viewed once with the greatest concentration, then filed away. Edge numbering was done by Vera, an ex-student who worked for a film company. I don't think I ever thanked her enough for the many hours she sat behind the viewer and meticulously scratched in the edge numbers.

Her boss, Rod Kinnear, generously helped me with two small films. It was the first time I had seen a professional at work. I learned an enormous amount from him. Rod also introduced me to Russell Hurley, a true traditionalist of the cinema who taught me some of his fine skills and how to discipline myself. Then there was a rather weird Dutchman called Eddie, who lived in my kitchen. I owe him a great deal. He could hardly spell his name, but had genius. He was not only a brilliant animator, but also one of the most inventive people I've ever met. He made his living cutting newsreel for a commercial station and we often sneaked into the station to use their equipment at night by bribing the cleaners. He shot and edited *Matuta* and *Time Past*.

Eddie possessed an old record player and three scratchy LP's: Handel's *Water Music*, parts of Mozart's Requiem and some eastern European folk songs. He played these records every night and all through the night when he was working on his clay sculptures or inventing new figures for his animation. One of these songs has never left me. I hum it regularly. Still to this day I don't know what the song is or where it came from. One day I will find out.

Robert Langley and Bill Frew, potters and sculptors, had moved into an old shop two houses down the road. Robert also played Handel's *Water Music* with large blobs of clay on the record. Many artists and would-be artists visited the studio. They came for classes in pottery or joined our weekly poetry readings. Bohemia had hit the suburbs. It was a wild time with wine, women and song and I went full blast into it. Australia had a very free spirit at the time. Nobody told you what to do, where to go, how to progress in work and love. I started to liberate myself from those dark shadows of the past. In this isolation I could pioneer, find my true instincts.

French troubadour and artist of life Jean-François Rogeon came to have some promotional photographs taken. Here we had a man who had travellled the world and survived brilliantly by performing on street corners and making quick watercolours of people's houses. A marvellous free spirit. Peter Tammer and Monique Schwartz set up shop next door. Peter made experimental films. He introduced me to his filmmaking friends and lent me his movie camera. He had wild ideas, untroubled by commercial demands and helped me greatly in finding a new home for my dreams.

Driving through the hills outside Melbourne one day, I came across a small sign that read 'Goats for Sale'. Without hesitation I purchased a small goat, loaded her in my car and made a home for her in the backyard. She was not happy with being relegated to the back, and was clever enough to install herself comfortably inside the house. I took her for walks in the park across the road. Wherever I went in my car, Rebecca had to go too. She was an excellent passenger and I'm sure — had I been patient enough — would have learned how to drive. If I went to a party, Rebecca would follow and automatically become the guest of honour. If she wasn't offered a snack, she would jump on the table and serve herself.

The trouble was, Rebecca grew bigger by the day. When she was almost the size of a donkey I had to accept Maudie Palmer's invitation to give Rebecca a new home on Maudie's parents' farm. It was a sad day, indeed, when I squeezed Rebecca into the car and drove her off to her new abode. She knew I was deserting her and for many hours refused to leave the car. Years later I visited her. She was now the size of a horse, but still remembered me and came galloping down the field. Who says goats are stupid?

Someone left a young puppy behind in my studio. The owner had disappeared by the time I could respond to the doorbell. After Rebecca this was not what I needed. However, I put her on trial, called her Thetis — the mother of Achilles — and for the next eighteen years Thetis was my steady companion and comrade-in-arms. She was a patient darkroom assistant and willing extra in several films.

Some fifteen years later I made a film for a seeing-eye dog school. The director, Phyllis Gration, had tried to train a dingo called Nerida to become a seeing-eye dog. For the first six months Nerida had been a brilliant student but then slowly lost interest in her career and started to fail her exams. She wasn't made for the workforce. Nerida came to live with us. I was married at the time and we were expecting our first child. In the beginning it was extremely difficult to look after Nerida. She kept urinating on our bed, ate the mail when she got a chance and chewed through any shoe or sandal she could find. People were terrified of her and I kept her out of sight as much as possible. Thetis, of course, felt a little left out. After all this was her territory. Fifteen years of serving and some upstart gets all the attention. But they soon shared bed and breakfast and were inseparable. Once I returned from a four-week trip and as I got out of the taxi in front of the house I could hear Nerida howling in the backyard. An ancient dark howl straight from the heart of Australia. When I came to greet her she was too overcome to move; then finally jumped into my arms. Thetis couldn't compete with that.

After my daughter's birth Nerida changed considerably. She adored the baby and, whenever she got the chance would curl up next to her. When Thetis was eighteen years old and could hardly walk the vet advised us to put her down. But Nerida stepped in. With one swift bite she killed her old mate. A true mercy killing.

A dear friend returned from the States and offered me a journey of sorts. LSD was something mysterious and needed to be investigated. We went to the seaside and indulged. As we made love, I saw my own birth and met my father in heaven. Two days later I returned to earth on the floor of a police cell in a country town.

At some stage I'd left the house we were staying in, convinced that I was God himself. Walking outside in the middle of the night, I removed all my clothes and flew off like a bird. I flew across ugly cities that, with one sweep of my hand, could be wiped off the map and replaced by thick forests. With my fingers, I drew silver rivers feeding from the ocean. With such glory and power on hand, it was obvious that I'd become God and was dying for the good of humanity. My father drifted by on a purple cloud. My mother called from across the mountains. My heart was pumping with such force that with every beat it jumped out of my chest and had to be caught before it hit the ground, then put back into my chest.

By now I'd reached the highway where early holiday-makers had appeared towing caravans. I came across a milkman and told him I was God and had come to die for him. He alerted the police. 'There's a naked man running along the highway. He claims to be God and wants to be taken to a hospital to save us and himself.' It had dawned on me by now that I could only be of use to the world if I stayed alive; I had to find a hospital where they could keep my heart in its place.

Three police cars appeared with a stunned police force who tried to corner me. I asked them to have respect, that I had an important message. I ran up a small hill and gave a speech in three different languages — this is what I was told later. When one policeman finally came close enough, I kissed this Judas on the mouth and had myself arrested.

I spent three days lying in jail under a dirty blanket until I was bailed out. Now and then someone would come to return an article of my clothing: a single sock, a pair of underpants, a shoe. My watch was found hanging from a tree.

A week later I went to court and heard the whole story. A chemist who was to explain to the court what LSD was, couldn't pronounce the words, and thus I was put on a good behaviour bond. The next day I read this on the front page of the local paper:

Naked in the Street
LSD charge fails

GEELONG — A Melbourne photographer under the influence of LSD ran naked through Anglesea, police told the City Court today.

But the man was acquitted on a charge of using the drug. He was put on a $20, 12 months' good-behaviour bond on a charge of offensive behaviour. Paul Henricus Cox, of Punt Road, South Yarra, pleaded not guilty to the charges. Sen. Constable Reginald George Sparling, of Anglesea, told the court that about 5.15am last Sunday he saw Cox walking naked along Ocean Road. He said Cox waved his arms, and said: 'I am God, I am God. I must find somewhere to die. I have to die for you.' He said Cox ran away, but he caught him. Sen. Constable Sparling said he told Cox he was under arrest. Cox said: 'Thank you' and tried to kiss him. Sen. Constable Sparling said Cox told him he had taken LSD. It was the first time ... Sen. Constable Sparling said Cox's clothes were found scattered around Anglesea. Cross-examined by Mr T. O'Brien, for Cox, Sen. Constable Sparling said Cox said later he had not realised he was running around naked ...

Another headline read: 'Photographer over-exposed ...'

That night I started to pack my bags to leave Australia for good. I felt deeply upset and humiliated, despite the fact that many friends thought this was very funny. As I carried my last suitcase down the stairs, there was an accident on the busy road in front of my studio. A small car had been pushed, driver and all, through the front window. He was still sitting, strapped in but unharmed, in his car, wearing a small, black hat. I stayed to clean up the mess. I stayed even longer to cope with all the extra work my sudden fame had brought me, and never again indulged in anything as silly and irresponsible as experimenting with drugs.

Australia also helped me to define that question, 'Where is home?' I was always homesick, but not for Holland or Europe. The space and vastness of this land has helped me to accept that I have no home. Homesickness is a strange disease. It stretches from the wilds of Borneo to the icy peaks of Alaska. The Germans call this particular brand of homesickness *fernweh*.

Throughout the years I've watched Australia trying to develop its own identity. In the process, slowly losing its uniqueness, its freedom, its wildness. The films I have made here could not have been made elsewhere. They have a European heart and are therefore more appreciated outside this country, but they're rooted here in this land of immigrants.

In Bali I sat mesmerised reading Patrick White's *The Vivisector*. I'd read most of his previous books, found his vision quite dazzling and his metaphysical concerns with Australia immensely intriguing — made all the more unique and profound by his deep understanding of European civilisation. I loved *The Vivisector* and wrote Patrick White a letter regarding a possible screen adaptation. I was amazed to get a reply. 'My experience of filmmaking (eight years and the film of *Voss* still not taking off) inclines me to avoid anything to do with it in future. Anyway, surely films from original scripts are more satisfactory than films from novels.' Of course he was right, but I wouldn't let the matter rest and over the next ten years, he kept sending me odd letters with scathing attacks on the people that had tried to make *Voss*.

He liked *Lonely Hearts* and after seeing *Man of Flowers* sent an amusing letter.

> I prefer *Lonely Hearts* because it is less kinky. But that doesn't mean *Man of Flowers* is not a memorable film, and Norman Kaye a superb actor and elegant man. So many wonderful moments. I lose count of them. The girl very appealing, some of the guest artists less so. Marianne Baillieu's purple boobs pretty appalling, but they are purple. I met her in the flesh a few nights before. Werner Herzog very much of the period. I could have done without Laurence Olivier's premature ejaculation. I am not normally one to carry on about bad taste, because I am inclined to commit it myself.

My love for the Australian soil has its roots in White's vision, his passionate understanding of this land. Apart from Grant Watson, no other European writer has ever so mystically penetrated the deeper secrets of this continent. People still ask me now: 'What do you actually think of Australia?' It always puzzles me, because this very question shows such insecurity. There's a difference here between the land and the people. Apart from the Aborigines, the people seem detached from the soil. There's no spiritual connection. Consequently, they've started more and more to imitate the rest of the Western world, instead of inventing their own country. They came here and conquered; imported European values and habits that have no home on this continent, forced the Aborigines off the land with great brutality and lack of respect. What a different country Australia would have become if the white men had observed and respected the Aboriginal spirit and followed the ancient call of the Dreaming.

All through the making of *The Journey* I was haunted by a short film I'd seen of Toscanini conducting *The Force of Destiny*. The film was used to promote an Italian 16mm projector for which my father had been given a franchise. I was totally spellbound when I first saw the film in our living room. I was probably about fourteen at the time. When the camera went out into the streets, travelled along telephone lines, across rooftops, into foreign cities, something snapped in me. I journeyed with the music, with Toscanini's mad passion, to unknown territories, into the deepest valleys and onto the highest mountain tops. Here was another reality at work, a reality I could understand and feel close to.

The script of *The Journey* changed with the weather. Every weekend I came up with major changes that were seriously discussed with my crew of two and the main lead, a wonderful man called Alan Money. Alan took the whole exercise even more seriously than I did. Chris and Maudie Palmer's daughter, Greta, was recruited to play a child who doesn't want to suffer a piano lesson and insists on a little dance with our protagonist. When he whirls around with her, she hits a vase with flowers, which causes great consternation to the mother. I hadn't learned then to treat the actors with respect, and played it for real. Greta was not impressed. I hope she has forgiven me by now.

Towards the end of shooting I spent three weekends driving through the country trying to film a rainbow. Why I needed this rainbow is not clear now, but at the time I couldn't have done without it.

The film was shown to a few friends, ignored by the people who mattered and put away. Doing the things one dreams of is more important, much more important, than enjoying the achievements.

In the process of making *The Journey*, I also realised that I could only learn the craft of film making by doing it, teaching myself. I didn't have the ability to learn from books or watch others who were not on the same wave length. Film seemed the ideal vehicle to give form and shape to those deeper layers that linger inside us. Later I discovered that the keys to these invisible doors are very close by. The birth of my daughter, for instance, the tears of my son, the end of my marriage, the death of my mother.

Meanwhile I had shot a small film in Greece with the help of my friend Jim Wilson. Jim was a quiet visionary, a wonderful, gentle soul and an extremely talented filmmaker. From him I learned the art of using super 8. His early death was a great loss, not only to his family and friends but also to the cinema.

It took more than a year before I could find the courage to put this film together. Most of the things that are clumsily touched upon in *The Journey* and further explored in *Island* have been re-explored in later work. *Island* is a ten-minute film about homesickness. It took six months to complete. The editing, and the many optical effects that were needed at the time, engrossed me totally. In this period I lost most of my friends and my lover. This ponderous poem, written on the island, was the backbone.

Your voice thru past and future memories ...
into a blurry mess of shattered stone.
Your eyes uncovering the bleeding wound inside my head ...
Faces I had known but didn't know ... hostile eyes
with smiles from twisted mouths.

Hands that caressed and touched my bones.

Welcome stranger this is your home.
Your future reposes on the cold cracking fingers
of death.

But the cool past opened up shy human friendships
among the ruins.

But I'm not a stranger.

Suddenly the sun and your immortal voice...whispering
close to me ... surrounding my skin with the greatest tenderness.
I remember your shadow and the painful sweetness
of your smile.

Then followed you thru narrow twisted streets.
a labyrinth of empty alleyways ...
your face bleached out thru centuries of burning light ...

Fear kept me alive as I stepped upon the blood drops of
murdered children ...

Suddenly your shadow ... or was it mine ... groping silently among
the things unknown.

Am I too passionate to die?

I found myself wandering around old buildings ... searching
thru the stone that so easily could have been my home.
Suddenly the bells and too much to celebrate ...
Thru the chaos of voices your shadow dancing in despair ...

But why then didn't you feel that soft singing of my blood ...
you never heard my silent voice ...
After all these centuries ... not one moment without your name upon
  my lips

But we sang and danced for an endless night
Too much happiness for a single soul

In the morning a hand came walking thru the storm ... Mother ...
And I remembered the bitter sweet taste of her milk
as she walked away from me —
ten thousand years ago.
But I saw you dear Mother ... and felt a little your
immense love ...

Suddenly a rose bursting into flame ...
cracking the fragile shell of my soul with its thorns.

The white spaces of the day touched the memory
of my innocence ... there was no limit to my ecstasy

But memory came back to me ...
too much had passed before my eyes ...

Then the endless waters called me back...
and once more I was drowned.

When the film was completed I realised that I wanted to be a filmmaker. That I needed to be a filmmaker. I was hooked.

Sixteen years later I returned to the same island to shoot a feature film, also entitled *Island*. It was the only way I could free myself from those obsessive visuals and re-examine the question: 'Where is home?'

'I make a humble attempt at being me', an Indian Sadhu once told me. He gave me a little book, *The Bhagavadgita* or 'The Song Divine'. In it I read:

> This is a book containing the highest esoteric doctrines. Its language is so sweet and simple that man can easily understand it after a little practice, but the thoughts are so deep that none can arrive at their end, even after constant study throughout a lifetime. Every day they exhibit new facets of truth, therefore they remain ever fresh and new.

I feel that the preface in *The Bhagavadgita* has a lot to do with film, with the true potential of the medium.

There are about five films that have never left me. Ingmar Bergman's *Persona*, for instance — and, as mentioned already, Paradjanov's *Shadows of our Forgotten Ancestors*. Also Jacques Tati's *Monsieur Hulot's Holiday* never fades from memory. Humour is always very personal when it touches upon our basic vulnerability and idiosyncrasies, it becomes the most intimate way to share our secret joys. I watch *Monsieur Hulot* at least once a year. It helps me to laugh at the world and at myself. I know of other films that somehow have burned a hole in my subconscious and are still travelling with me. So film must have the potential to remain forever *fresh and new*. Only in retrospect do we discover this.

Small things often haunt us. The smile of a child, a bird in flight, a patch of light on the wall, a face in the crowd. Slight brushstrokes that linger and last. Unfortunately we are saturated with images flashing at us from all directions. Images of a consumer society, that have no past and no substance. Images that do not feed our dreams or our imagination.

When one of the English journalists captured by the Iraqis during the Gulf War was asked what he thought of during his ordeal in an Iraqi jail, he said, with tears in his eyes, 'The little moments in life ...When I went for a walk in Normandy in the French countryside with a beautiful French girl who later became my wife ... When I held my daughter's hand and we walked along the beach.'

Those really important moments. They have nothing to do with the usual violence and violation one encounters in so many films. These moments are drenched with humanity, with human feelings. with longing and hope and, above all, with our dreams. Just imagine if someone dared today to have the idea of making a film called *Forbidden Games (Jeux Interdits)*, René Clement's great film about two children stealing crosses for their own cemetery. I saw it some forty years ago. It had a lasting effect on me and I'm sure had much to do with my future direction. Who would fund a film of such humble greatness in our present climate?

Time is our true judge. Birth and death are separated by a leaf falling in autumn, a cloud passing by, a bird in flight, a train hurrying through the night, a smile, a tear, the pain of too much tenderness.

To appreciate a good painting, one has to look at it for a long time. Nothing can trigger or stimulate the heart and the imagination when the impression is 'fast and painless'. I have to call on the writing of van Gogh again to clarify this. He wrote about his *Sunflowers*: 'You can exhibit the picture of my sunflowers. You will see that this is the kind of painting that rather changes to the eye and takes on richness the longer you look at it.'

Vincent also told a friend with whom he visited the Rijksmuseum in Amsterdam that he wanted to sit in front of Rembrandt's *The Jewish Bride* for a few weeks in order to study it properly. But in Arles he screams out:

> Everyone will say that I work too fast. Don't you believe a word of it. Is it not emotion, the sincerity of one's feelings for nature that draws us, and if the emotions are sometimes so strong that one works without knowing one works, when sometimes the strokes come with a continuity and a coherence like words in a speech or a letter, then one must remember that it has not always been so and that in time to come there will be hard days empty of inspiration; so one must strike when the iron is hot and put the forged bars on one side.

One can only come to this purification of one's emotion and passion through an attempt at self-discipline, yet at the same time one must allow an undisciplined passion to flourish. In India I learned a little about time and timelessness and despite my general impatience with things, a little about stillness. India helped me to think for myself. To look at the world without getting lost in trivialities.

INDIA

India vibrates with music. It's offered freely and openly and most musicians and singers in the villages are a lot more talented than the average Western pop celebrity. It's strange and disconcerting at times to find such melodious beauty in the villages, the slums of Calcutta, Bombay or New Delhi or amongst the poorest stone cutters in Kerala.

In Calcutta, together with an American teacher called Sheila, I went to a lecture on Rabindranath Tagore at the Calcutta University, which had been advertised in a local newspaper. While waiting in the crowd we met a young poet, Anil Acharya. We never got to the lecture: we talked, read poetry and sang songs until the early morning as if we'd been friends for years. Anil and I became brothers. When I was planning to make *Island* so many years later, Anil gave me a record of Tagore songs. One song in particular haunted me constantly ... I didn't understand the words but decided to use the music in the film. It somehow felt right. It's usually a difficult and expensive task to get the copyright for existing music, but with Anil's help, the song was provided gratis by the Tagore Society and the singer Ritu Guha.

She said: 'It's an honour for me to contribute to your film, to combine our artistic endeavours. Thank you so much.' One can't possibly imagine such a response, such a precious gift, coming from any of the more 'developed' countries. A large bill would precede a large contract. Anil translated the devotional song:

> *Why do I by chance see you?*
> *Why not always and every day?*
> *Why do black clouds appear*
> *in my heart that prevent*
> *me from seeing you?*
> *Whenever I blink my eyes*
> *I cannot see you. I'm afraid*
> *I'd lose you and lose you*
> *suddenly.*
> *Tell me what I have to do*
> *to touch you and to always*
> *keep you in my eyes.*
> *Where can I gather so much*
> *love, to stay in your*
> *heart?*
> *I'll never look at anyone.*
> *Here I lay my heart.*
> *You only have to ask and*
> *I'll sacrifice all my earthly*
> *desires.*

I think my real growing up happened in India. I've returned many times — sometimes without telling Anil and his wife Sahana as they were always so hospitable that it was hard to leave them for other parts of India. I needed to explore the whole of the Indian continent, remain a stranger, talk to strangers. In India I lost my fears; my heart opened up. Despite its raging poverty and terrible injustice, India is a giving place. People who have nothing insist on sharing. They give willingly, they bleed willingly, without making a face. My films travel well in this country. They are accepted and understood. The Indians have an instinctive sense of humour and a natural acceptance of their inadequacies.

After so many visits and much time spent on this continent, I still know nothing about India. I remain ignorant of her and treasure this ignorance. I never looked at a tourist guide or gathered information before a visit to a certain place or district. Always felt too overcome, too dumbfounded by India's all-embracing spirit and the individuality of its people. But I wonder at times why I remember with such clarity that evening drifting in a small boat on the Ganges. The early morning dew like a blanket of tiny diamonds in Andhra Pradesh. That golden fish jumping in a murky pond in Bengal or the slender trees that grace the mountains near Dharjeeling.

I also wonder why so many people remain engraved in my heart. Why the faces of the children travel with me. Why India gives me hope and peace and keeps reminding me that life, after all, must be an act of love, whatever the consequence.

Once I visited a small village in the south. I'd walked for many miles and was tired and ill. The local teacher offered me a little hut at the back of his house. I gratefully went to sleep and woke up a few hours later with a terrible pain in my chest — found it hard to breath. For days I drifted in and out of consciousness. The local doctor paid a daily visit on his ancient bicycle. He had no idea what was wrong with me, but after each visit I felt better. He simply chanted for a while to chase the evil spirits away.

The daughter of the schoolmaster was given the job of keeping an eye on me. Dear, sweet woman — so shy, so delicate. When my health improved and I started to go down to the river to wash myself, she'd follow from a distance with a piece of cloth to be used as a towel. As soon as I'd finished, the cloth would be lying on the grass nearby, with no sign of her. When I'd fully recovered and tried to pay for the expense, these very poor people wouldn't hear of it; instead, they gave me presents and food for the journey ahead. The schoolmaster's daughter wept so hard that in defiance of local custom I embraced her. For an instant I felt infinitely close to her.

Thirty years later I went back to this region, tried to find this village again; but it seemed to have become part of the town. The river was still there with the ancient, slow-moving boats and that shimmering evening light, but I couldn't locate the village. The mud huts and shanty houses had been replaced with ugly concrete blocks and the people had vanished.

I took *The Nun and the Bandit* to the film festival in Delhi. I'd persuaded the distributor to have the premiere in India — no one else had shown much enthusiasm and our local exhibitor had already returned all the prints without bothering with a release. A little disappointing, to say the least. On the day of the grand premiere, I was awakened at six in the morning by a police officer and an elderly official. 'Good morning, Mr Cox. We have very bad news for you.' I had been drinking rum with film students until four in the morning and wasn't ready for any news. 'Very bad news indeed.' They walked into my room and made themselves comfortable; bad news travels slowly here.

'We're terribly sorry. You must be very upset, Mr Cox.'

'I'll be very upset if you don't tell me what's happened.'

The official got up from the bed, lit a cigarette and announced: 'Your film has been taken last night and copied. That's our conclusion. There are tapes of 'Bandit and his Nuns' all over town.' The phone rings with the same news; the girl on the phone gets the title right.

That night there was a special atmosphere in the cinema. The audience was curious about my reaction to what had been happening. The cinema was packed and a packed cinema in India is something to be experienced. Not just every available seat was taken; the majority of the audience was sitting, lying or standing on every inch of the floor.

In my best Indian accent, I told the audience about the two gentlemen in the morning, 'The Bandit and his Nuns' with the bad tidings. Then I thanked the 'pirates' for their trouble and for having introduced my film to a larger public. 'I don't make my films for myself — unfortunately, they only appeal to a small audience — and I'm very pleased that you've helped me here to find a larger audience.' I meant it. There was much laughter and applause and the next night the film was shown on Indian television with the largest audience I could ever hope for.

It's hard to believe that India has the largest film industry in the world. Eight or nine hundred films a year are being made in twenty-five languages and dialects.

To join an Indian audience in an ordinary cinema, watching an ordinary, commercial Hindi film, is an amazing experience. It can be troublesome to follow the plot, but I go for the atmosphere, watch the participation of the audience. Once I sat next to a gentleman who'd told me before the lights went down, that this was the greatest film ever and that he'd seen it already 23 times. He knew all the songs by heart and loudly anticipated what the stars were going to say on the big screen. I finally had to position myself elsewhere, as the audience around us was getting hostile. People make a lot of noise whilst watching children are allowed to run up and down the aisles, but to preamble what happens on the screen is a mortal sin. He was finally removed to a standing position in the back.

The alternative Indian cinema is of considerable originality and depth. Bengali masters like Satyajit Ray, Ritwik Ghatak and the still active and remarkable Mrinal Sen made truly indigenous films. Buddhadeb Dasgupta follows that tradition in Bengal with his tender and poetic films. Few will remember John Abraham, the ingenious brooding volcano who died far too early. Director Shyam Benegal is now one of the most important voices; and in the south there is Adoor Gopalakrishnan, an intimate storyteller whose *Elippathayam* is a profoundly moving masterpiece. But right across India there are thousands of young, dedicated filmmakers who, in spite of the enormous difficulties they face in finance and distribution, continue to keep a concerned indigenous film industry alive. They don't talk about who they're going to cast and what audience they have in mind. They talk about what they want to say and how to share their hopes and dreams with the people.

Then there was Aravindan, the holy man of Kerala, who died in 1990 of a massive heart attack. How this quiet giant, with his long white hair and beard, could die of a heart attack remains a mystery. Aravindan always popped up somewhere. We were silent friends, hardly exchanged a word; or, if there was anything to be said, I did the talking. His indefinite concept of time was hypnotic in his presence and in his films. His language was the language of faces. His respect for the individual spoke many languages. I was interviewed for a documentary on his life and films, and in true homage to this wonderful man, should just have stared at the camera without saying anything.

My first impression of Calcutta was so overwhelming that I returned the next year to make a short documentary. It was in the time of the Nexalites, young Communists who tried to change the system and were brutally suppressed. A general state of anxiety made filming in the streets quite harrowing; shooting from the hip was the only solution. We always had an escape route worked out before entering new territory and, with Anil, I ran through the crowded streets in anticipation of the worst.

I had a fixed focus wind-up camera with a turret and a small cassette recorder, bought at the airport. We had 14x100-foot rolls of 16mm film, which meant that virtually everything shot had to be used. Despite our few resources, this film had to be made. I had to record the terrible contrasts in a city that was known as hell on earth.

We were invited to the opening of an exhibition of sculpture. The gallery was in the heart of Calcutta and many guests had stepped over the bodies on the footpath to enter the gallery. It seemed strange that there was still money and time to celebrate the arts. A man with piercing black eyes singled me out of the crowd and said slowly: 'This is no time to pick flowers.'

India is not a land of lethargic gloom and doom. The Indian character is neither lethargic nor unhappy. No doubt there is cruelty and oppression, but in India the individual is still quietly celebrated and is the end product of that society. This can't be said about the West, where people are taught by their society to become above all good consumers.

An Indian artist once told me that he preferred the animal in him to the human being, because when the animal in him ran rampant, he felt a sense of belonging to the human race. As a human being he felt alone and separate. The human race disgusted him. 'Animals have remained animals and therefore live in harmony with nature. They consume only what is necessary', he said.

One day we saw hundreds of dead bodies piled up against the walls of the railway station. From all the dead I will always remember

With Anil Acharya in Calcutta.

one face: the face of an old man, his eyes wide open, silver hair like a crown around his head, his mouth like the Buddha. His eyes gazed beyond me with infinite tenderness. Later, when we returned from the country and our car was stopped by some trigger-happy soldiers, I had a flash of my own death and saw the old man smiling.

This was a harrowing experience. Two nervous soldiers pulled us out of our car screaming that they had the authority to shoot anyone crossing the bridge. Where did we come from? Who were we? What were we doing? One of my friends had a small pass which showed that he was a government official. The soldiers didn't trust this — or couldn't read — but were unsettled enough to wait for an officer to arrive. It was the longest hour of my life, standing in the heat facing the firing squad. When they finally let us go, we drove back to Calcutta in total silence, holding hands and smiling at the landscape.

Once I landed in Bangalore with terrible stomach problems.

> Dear Lord Krishna, where's the toilet? Please help. I find the toilet. Too late ... I'm in big trouble. Fortunately, there's a clean pair of underpants in my bag. The dirty pair goes into the toilet bowl. 'Goodbye and Amen.' Of course the system becomes blocked. How stupid. The water just stops at the top. Praying is all that can save me, but I can't kneel down. The floor is too dirty. I turn, hit the unattached toilet seat which skits into the next cubicle, comes to a halt against the feet of another customer. The man kindly pushes it back in my direction. I explode again, now squatting on top of the toilet. There is only one thing to be done — remove the underpants from the bowl. I close my eyes, dig deep into the darkest pit. Suddenly a growl from underneath the earth. My underpants disappear. An enormous force pulls them out of my hand. 'Thank you Lord Krishna, you've saved me.' I flush the toilet several times to wash my hand, replace the seat. I'm ready to face the world again. There are many pairs of feet waiting outside. They must know what's going on in here. I'll

be fast — run for cover. As I open the door and grab my bag, there's a disturbing noise coming from deep within the toilet bowl. Together with a spellbound audience I see the toilet erupt. The seat shoots off like a frisby and my underpants fly through the air. The man next door screams. People run for cover. I escape into the crowded street and offer a taxi driver a small fortune to rush me to the best hotel in town.

I found these images in my notebook of my first visit to Calcutta. Crows cry outside my window. Down below, a busy street with car horns and voices. Inside my room, an old fan is painfully protesting against the current. Calcutta, city of life, of old, ancient ruins. City of death. Even new buildings appear old in this place. The sweetest happiness and the greatest pain all have the one face. On a wall, I read:

> *So this is all*
> *but you and I*
> *we counted on a thousand years.*

Then: 'Learn English, we teach you. We improve your future, you live longer. No more confusion.'

I suddenly feel so lonely that a simple smile can break my heart. Towards the end, Tagore said: 'I have loved this life and because of that I shall love death as well'. Yes, we must come to death in peace and harmony, otherwise there's no point in living nor in dying.

I buy a bottle of Coke to clear the dust from my throat. On the footpath, an old piece of canvas. A hand emerging from one side, and part of a foot. As I approach, I find another hand and a bare skull. Flies are wandering in and out, and high above our heads a silent vulture. People are rushing by. The Coca Cola man demands his bottle back. Nearby, a little boy rolls across the footpath, his feet neatly amputated, although the shape of one stump seems a little longer than the other. A man touches my arm. 'You want change money, sir? I give you good rate.' The little boy rolls past my feet. I think of my child ...

Now the night has come. A grey, black sky hovers over the city. Beggars lie curled up under dirty blankets and sleep alone. Children cry nearby and a lonely old man calls in the distance. Next door, a woman starts to sing to her child. 'Sleep well, my little one, sleep. The sun will wake you if you sleep, so close your eyes and sleep.'

We talk about reincarnation. I can't believe in the reincarnation of the individual soul. We belong to one great mind and while travelling through our lives, living this conscious state, we must create positive action to be of use to others in this and future lives. I don't care if I return as part of a flower, rock or tree. I'm part of this great power manifestation and therefore timeless and infinite.

A mosquito net protects me, but there's no sleeping. I listen to every single sound of the night — separate each one. Put them into their own world. There's harmony and yet every sound has its own clarity, separately, like paint on a canvas. It's up to me to compose the symphony. But I feel lost in this vastness — so immensely insignificant.

I'm waiting at the airport in Madras. I've been delayed for six, eight, ten hours, maybe more. I'm not worried. One can only write about India when one is actually here, yet when one is here, one is too dumbfounded to speak. A woman in blue is sweeping the floor. When she finishes, she goes back to the beginning. Who is this woman? What are her thoughts? She only pays attention to children and smiles at them. Through a dirty window, the evening glow of an Indian sun. Huge clouds are collecting pink, blue, orange, purple, then drift into the dark.

Many years ago, when I parted from Anil, he said: 'When I weep for us, I also weep for my country. You must return.' I've always come back here. I feel at home.

Now I'm sitting in a quiet hotel room in Trivandrum with an extraordinary view over the ocean. The flea-ridden rooms of my early travels to India have disappeared. I miss them. Apart from the distant rock music, I'm in paradise. Tagore's words return: 'I keep gazing on the far-away gloom of the sky and my heart wanders, wailing with the restless wind'. In the West we are forced, or pushed away from 'the reality of the distance'.

The ocean in front of me is real. Yet I can only comprehend its vastness by keeping my eyes fixed on a distant fishing boat. I gaze at this 'mirage' a long time, then close my eyes. Now I see everything much more clearly.

I remember when my mother lost her sight. I came home from school and found her surrounded by members of the family, neighbours and a doctor. She'd suddenly gone blind. Later, when I visited her in hospital, she was lying peacefully in a little room with pale green walls. She couldn't see my tears, but felt them. 'I can still *see into the distance*, well beyond it. Please don't be upset. It's very peaceful here,' she said. She had no idea that her sight would be restored, but her courage gave me hope and her peace had a great visionary aura. This planted the seeds for the film *Cactus*.

Most things don't function in India — and why should they? I have two telephones in my apartment, but I've come to realise that a telephone is only there to make you feel at home. You must not expect it to work. As soon as you accept this fact, you understand a little about India. I'm writing this with a pencil left in my room on which is written, *With compliments ... Hotel President, Bombay. It's nice to love people.* How can anyone not love India?

My friend and agent, Mrs Seawell, is staying in the same hotel. I try to ring out for two hours, but cannot get through. I finally try, via the operator, to get put through to Mrs Seawell's room. The following dialogue develops:

- Mrs Seawell's room, please.
- See what?
- Seawell, please.
- I see. [*Pause.*] There's no Mrs Sea.
- Excuse me, I didn't ask for Mrs Sea, I would like to speak to Mrs Seawell. Jeannine Seawell.
- There's no Mrs Jeannine here ... We have a Miss Well ...
- No, I want Seawell. S-E-A-W-E-L-L.
  Long pause. I hear him talking to someone. He returns to the phone.
- Excuse me, could you ring back in an hour or two, please? Thank you very much.
  He hangs up. For a while I sit very quietly. I mustn't get upset. The phone rings.
- Mr Seawell? [*Before I can utter a word*] What is the number of your room, please?
- 007 [*I joke.*]
- Thank you very much.
  He hangs up.

I go to the lobby and ask to see the operator. They direct me through a narrow corridor into a small room with an ancient telephone exchange. My operator friend sits behind it, wearing Bakelite earphones. He's enthusiastically plugging extensions in and out at random. A trainee assistant watches him with admiration.

- Excuse me, I'm the person who tried to get through to Mrs Seawell's room. Have you worked it out yet?
- Oh ... you're Mr Seawell ... You gave me the wrong number.
  He produces a piece of paper on which is written "See-wel-007".

> You see? Please ... here it is.
> - I see!
> - We have a Miss Well here ...
>> *The exchange starts to buzz.*
> - New York? He's not here ... no ...
> - From New York?
> - He's from New York?
> - You are from New York?
>> *He looks around. What to do next?*
> - Can you ring back in an hour, please?
> - Yes, please.

At this point I decide to leave and in the lobby walk straight into Mrs Seawell. I try to explain, but fail miserably.

The next morning there's a knock at the door. A smiling Indian greets me.

> - Good morning. Sarah Miles?
>> *We both look round the room.*
> - No.
> - Is Sarah in, please?
> - I'm sorry, you must have ...
> - Could you please give this to her?
>> *He holds out an envelope.*
> - But she's not here. I ...
> - She's gone out?
> - I'm sorry, I don't know her.
> - It's all right ... I come back ... okay?
>> *He smiles and leaves me stunned, holding the envelope.*

Sarah Miles, of course, occupied the room before I arrived.

Years later in Delhi at yet another festival, a similar thing happened.

- Could you get me Miss Seawell's room?
- Her name is not in the computer ... kindly hold on ...
   The man hangs up. I try again. This time a woman's voice.
- Is Seawell the last or first name?
- Jeannine Seawell.
- Jeannine?
- No, that's the first name.
- Yes, but Seawell is not here.
- Well, Jeannine will do if you can find her.
- I'm putting your request into the information counter.
   After some distorted music the phone disconnects. I try again. No one answers for a long time. Finally, a thin voice. I presume it to be a man.
- Seawell?
- Yes ...
- You see well?
- Yes, I do. Please let me spell it for you. It's a surname — S-E-A-W-E-L-L.
- Yes, but what's the name?
- Seawell.
- Ah, that's a name we have in the computer, room 659.
- Thank you.
- Thank you very much.

Jeannine has come to realise that the Indian psyche somehow can't cope with her name. When she hits the Indian continent now, she calls herself Jeannine and all is well.

I've returned for a few days to Nepal. Kathmandu still has some remarkable corners where the light glows with great force. Years ago I published a little book called *Human Still Lives from Nepal*.

The preface was written here on one of these corners as the evening light filled the street with incantatory shadows:

> Sometimes we come across a ray of light falling through a narrow window or a dark hole above. Suddenly light speaks to us and for a moment lifts the dark veil from our fragmented existence. We are offered a glimpse into the nature of this world as it really is and all we have to do is watch in stillness. Stillness is the understanding of what is. We are all rays of light, falling helplessly through the dark pit of this life. Sometimes, however, these rays of light cross and suddenly there is inner light, with transparent walls and doors. The keys to these doors are the simple things we have to look at, without pretension, not acting a part, nor trying. Human still lives are silent images of light. We are as real as this light and in some ways even more infinite.

I'm re-establishing a friendship here that has, throughout the years, been more or less a religious bond, a worshipping of what van Gogh called 'that white light'. Friendship is like a religion, or more than that. And religion is an abstracted nature worship.

The ancient Greeks understood this. In a little book I read that religion has its origin in the personification of the powers of nature. Either man goes to seek the spirits of his ancestors, the spirit of the dead, or he needs to understand the power working behind the stupendous phenomena of nature. Whatever the case, he tries to transcend the limitations of the senses. The senses don't satisfy him. In the end he needs to go beyond and the first glimpse of all this comes through dreams. In fact I think that God speaks to us through dreams and visions, not through religion. Therefore the most profound religion of them all is the Dreaming.

Children know that there's little difference between their dreaming and their awakened state. During sleep the body is apparently dead, yet the mind goes on with all its intricate workings.

Don't the same workings go on after the body has been dissolved forever? Or does the soul escape when the flesh dies? If souls do not die, why then do we make so much of saying goodbye? People die in their sleep. Do their dreams travel on after death?

Once I left on a journey that would keep me on the road for at least a year. The night before departure I dined with a girl I'd known for some time. She drove me home in her battered old Volkswagen and we parted with a friendly kiss. Some weeks later, in Indonesia, I started to dream about her. In India I still dreamed about her. She always appeared in rooms filled with light. She would look at me and speak in a strange language. I felt an urgent need to contact her, to talk with her. Alas, there was no address. I wrote to a friend, asking him to pass on the letter. When I finally arrived in Europe there was a sweet letter from her waiting for me. We started to correspond. The dreaming ceased. I had fallen madly in love with her.

When I returned to Australia she was there at the airport, with all the light and tenderness of those dreams. We treasured each other for a full year. One night, this 'woman of my dreams' looked up and said: 'I'm leaving you.' It devastated me to such a degree that I spent the next six months staring through the back window at the weedy garden. Many, many years later I met her again. She wept right through lunch, and still couldn't answer my question: 'Why did you leave me?'

At least twice a year I have a dream about the 'house of my dreams'. A recurring dream, always with great clarity. It's a large house, on the edge of a small town, with a field of green in front and a small forest on one side. Throughout the years, I've seen this house being divided into apartments, and then restored to its old glory. I don't know which country it stands in, what language is being spoken. There are steps on either side of the door at the back, and down below, under the stairs, an entrance to the cellars.

There's a garden, overgrown with flowers and weeds and old plants; and a pathway and a small square with cobblestones. On either side, upstairs, a row of windows. The house is old and solid, some cracks have appeared high upon the walls. Does this house exist? Have I seen it somewhere on my wanderings and buried its memory in my subconscious? But I've been inside ... seen the long winding staircase in the entrance hall leading to the first and second floors. I've sat in the kitchen, watched the light play on the old fashioned stove and on the tiles that reach the ceiling. Where is this house?

While I was editing *Vincent*, my daughter Kyra slept upstairs above the editing room. After she had gone to bed, I would sneak down the stairs to the editing room and work on the film. I had Kyra linked up to a cheap intercom system in case she woke up and her breathing became an intricate part of my nightly endeavours. Often I heard her talking in her sleep. Amazing stories filtered through that started to make perfect sense to me, once I let go.

Our discussions over breakfast were remarkable. Usually she would not remember her dreams, but once I had reminded her of some remarks, she would pick up the thread, relive her dreams and often continue the journey.

'On the threshold of sleep I face unbearable tenderness.' Kyra's ability to move in and out of reality helped me greatly with the editing of *Vincent*. She was also responsible for the opening shot in *Cactus*. We stayed overnight at the location before shooting and, as night was closing in, we decided to go for a walk in the thick bushes that surrounded us. The many unfamiliar sounds of the night scared my little girl. Suddenly she stopped, pointed at the sky and said: 'Isn't it great, Daddy, the sky is everywhere.' She squeezed my hand tightly as if to say: 'We have a roof, we're not alone, I'm quite safe here.' It was a large, marvellous, all-embracing thought of which only children are capable.

The opening shot of *Cactus* rolls on and on, through valleys and mountains, forests and skies, completing a full circle. At this moment the appearing car penetrates the circle, the eyeball. A metaphor for the eye (vision) has been established and the sliver of glass that will eventually destroy the light in Isabelle Huppert's eye.

The first time I came to Nepal I felt a great sense of relief, a new freedom opened up. Wounds a long time covered started to bleed again and finally cleanse themselves. A friend who had finished his career as a doctor had become a Buddhist monk and persuaded me that I, too, should try to find Buddha. I did join the many devotees that sat around a very fine and wise Tibetan lama, but could only bear it for a limited time. I needed to be alone to find whatever I was looking for.

Then a Thai monk asked me to join him on a small visit to a monastery in the mountains. We first returned to Kathmandu, then set out on foot with some chocolate and two flasks of water. He was a kind and gentle soul with limited English, maybe a few years older than I. We walked for two days, slept in a small hut and arrived at a strange looking temple tucked away in a mountain cave.

I have never been able to work out exactly how long we stayed there. I was virtually a prisoner of circumstance. My friend the monk went into a deep state of meditation. The other monks were well beyond approach. All I could do was share their smiles and watch them chant and pray.

The first week I went half-mad with fear and loneliness. I missed the world, my family, my friends, my music, my books, my life. Then I started to realise that none of these were mine, that for this time I belonged there, and I started to look at the landscape, at the sky, away from my own anxieties. I started to live.

I also felt something growing inside, much stronger than I, much more appealing. On scraps of paper I made notes:

Carefully she looked at me
carefully she smiled
carefully she vanished

We're the guests of summer fields
and shall be here forever ...

A yellow tree
A purple bird
What ecstacy

God came to me out of the woods
and I became a poet

A child kissed me
and I blushed

I remember her
so soft, so silent
when she spoke

Shadows slowly kiss the earth
embrace the night
embrace and hide

Dancing water drowned your voice
bu I heared sweet laughter when
I washed that night

Silver, gold and blue
One stray white cloud
Silver, gold and blue

Every single blade of grass a mystery
too sacred to be touched

A mountain celebrates with roaring laughter
I am beautifully alone

We shall always meet
because we love

Every day I grew smaller and the landscape in front grew larger. Then many paintings I had admired appeared with great clarity. I finally settled on Vermeer. Somehow Vermeer was more infinite than others, yet his universe came from his own backyard. I tried to remember his paintings as accurately as possible. Composition, colour, light. Especially the light. When my Thai friend came to ask me: 'You ready?' I said: 'Yes'. He said: 'Strong?' I said: 'Yes'. Then he said: 'Journey starting now.'

We returned to Kathmandu. My friend simply vanished and I found myself in a dollar-a-night hotel on the second floor, overlooking a narrow street. That night a small group of musicians came strolling down the laneway. From the far distance I could hear the approaching bells, flutes and chanting. They stopped in front of a small shrine situated right in front of my window. They stood there, they played, they chanted, they prayed. Centuries passed between my window and that street. As they continued down the alleyway playing their ancient instruments, my last drop of blood travelled with them.

As soon as I arrived in Holland I made a pilgrimage to the

Rijksmuseum in Amsterdam. I needed to match the imprint in my mind with some real Vermeers. It was a very moving homecoming. The isolation in the mountains had shaped a fairly precise memory of the exterior of the paintings. But the real images were now so solid, so far reaching, so immensely beautiful. The paintings were pulsating within me. There was so much more to be discovered behind the paintings. My eyes had been allowed to explore, to remember, find poetry and light, look inwards.

India is the land of the unexpected, of poetry, mystery and mysticism. One day, Ulli Beier showed me a few slides he'd taken of Nek Chand's Rock Garden in Chandigarh. Within a few weeks we were on our way to make a little film about this extraordinary creation.

Nek Chand, a humble man, was working as a road inspector near Chandigarh when he had a vivid dream of a vast kingdom on the very site of which he was in charge. For the next eight years he ventured to convert this wasteland into the magic kingdom of his dream. Working day and night after normal working hours, he gathered and transported on his bicycle stones, rocks and urban waste. He retrieved old cycles and unusable parts from cycle shops. He burned old bicycle tyres to give him light at night. He collected used factory drums and broken crockery from restaurants and cafes. He collected buckets full of broken bangles thrown away after festivals. Out of all this garbage, broken articles of daily use, pebbles and stones, he built his kingdom.

Beginning with the king's throne, the original dream expanded. The garden grew and grew, quietly, never requiring the purchase of materials, subsidy or advice. Art for art's sake, for no reward, no recognition during the long years in solitude.

The garden remained a secret until it was discovered eight years after its conception by government employees spraying against malaria on the outskirts of the city. The discovery so moved officials that they began to help Nek Chand. Some politicians complained about a government employee using public land, but this narrow-mindedness was soon ignored. The Rock Garden was formally inaugurated in 1976 and since then people from all over the world have visited this strange, almost living work of art. A wonderland of rare artistic merit created entirely from waste material. The director of the Musée de l'Art Moderne in Paris wrote in Nek Chand's visitor's book, 'God has a competitor — his name is Nek Chand.'

No visitor entering this magic garden remains unmoved. Children gaze enthralled; adults are mesmerised. This is the work of a single obsessive human being, an artist of great instinctive integrity. I've watched people visiting Disneyland, and I've sat for days high on the wall of Nek Chand's kingdom, watching its visitors. No doubt Disneyland is enchanting, but the people leave spiritually empty-handed. Here in Nek Chand's garden they are enriched to such a degree that they leave quietly, holding hands, smiling. They've shared something of magic and beauty that will nourish their dreams for many years to come.

The United States

Nowadays I'm spending more time in the United States than in the so-called underdeveloped countries. Once again I've been tempted to 'try Hollywood' and sit here wasting my time and energy. But my adopted country, Australia, doesn't always allow me to continue making films. Work continuity as such doesn't exist. Even after making many feature films, the same battle to assemble the money has to be fought each time.

I'm here to discuss the making of my first American adventure ... I know that the whole exercise is already doomed, but will have to stay a few more days so as not to disappoint the few worthwhile people amongst the many rats that call themselves movie producers ...

This morning I met one of them: intelligent, youngish, impeccably dressed. A large modern desk with nothing on it. What's an empty desk doing in a busy life?

'If we want to communicate human truths, we must use the language of poetry and not the language of reason,' I suggested with some cheek.

'That's exactly right, Paul. Glad you think that way, but I was talking about compromise. Not for our sake, but for the public's sake.'

Yes, everything seems to end up as compromise, and compromise is only another name for failure.

The big studios don't really make films. From a 'project' it becomes part of a 'package' and then a movie. Anything unfamiliar or original that treats the human condition in any depth is out. The studio needs to feel safe and would much rather spend big on something stupid than a little on something worthwhile. A lot of people I meet here have never sweated movies and reserve their enthusiasm for films that make money. Films that make money are good films.

Americans live in a free country, yet right here on my table I read: '*To ensure complete privacy, please lock your door ... As an additional security, please use the chain ... As an extra precaution ...*'

Yes, this is America. The people here in Los Angeles live in jails, be it a hotel room or a private home. On television nothing but the constant rape of our dignity, our basic humanity. I can watch on my television screen what will happen if I don't double-lock my door and make myself a prisoner.

I've stayed in little flea pits in the East where life is cheap, as they say, where people are not afraid of one another. Where they smile at you in the streets. Where you're absolutely safe day and night. The West calls these countries 'underdeveloped'.

On television an amazing program — a celebration of physical beauty, ignoring the fact that spiritual beauty is easier to achieve. Every cliché in the book: 'The eye of the beholder', 'Skin deep' etc. Then a parade of 'beautiful people'. Despite my irritation, I realise that I, too, am terribly sensitive to physical beauty. I'm not interested in the latest fashion or make-up tricks, but when I'm in a physical or spiritual wasteland, I shape a sort of artificial paradise on earth.

I make a cathedral out of a tent or an opera house out of a dingy hotel room; and, when there's nothing that can possibly delight the senses or the heart, I dig a hole into the earth and sulk.

I'm staying in a hotel with a 'non-smoking' floor. This might be a little hard for outsiders to understand, but one floor in the hotel is kept 'pure' and even in your own room you're not allowed to smoke. Of course I've landed on the wrong floor and have already been reprimanded by one of the porters. Now I'm puffing away on my pipe and hope and pray that my smoke will not drift through the double-locked door into the corridor. Smoking here in the States has become one of the capital sins. I wish the same energy, or rather hatred, would be directed towards drug taking or unfriendliness or violence, for that matter. Why there isn't a label on every gun saying: 'Danger — This gun is a health hazard' remains a mystery.

Last year when I was here I wrote the following reminiscence, which is the whole truth and nothing but ...

> I like to smoke. For over thirty years I've been steadily biting my way through many pipes. Pipe smokers are different from cigarette smokers and very different from non-smokers. Pipe smokers are more balanced, more at peace than cigarette smokers and much more relaxed than non-smokers. The pipe becomes a friend, a comrade in arms, a faithful companion.
>
> For some reason we are not allowed to smoke on planes now, which is a great injustice. In the old days one could have a few secret puffs in the lavatory, but since they installed smoke alarms, this has become too dangerous. Almost got caught once, sitting quietly unaware on the toilet seat. One delightful puff was enough to set off the alarm. In great panic I returned to my seat and hid under my blanket. (Fortunately it was night and everyone was asleep.) All hell had broken loose, with stewards and pilots running everywhere. I'm glad to report that they didn't catch me.

The worst place for pipe smokers is California. Most Californians are non-smokers. A smoker in California is an outcast, a public enemy. Popping pills or sniffing coke is much more acceptable. A few restaurants still have smoking sections but even there one is not safe. On several occasions I have been brutally reprimanded by puritans who were deeply offended by my pipe. One of these encounters is worth recalling.

During a lunch on the pier along the Santa Barbara Boulevard, a man behind me suddenly abused me for ruining his lunch. With Bill Marshall and two Hollywood agents I was sitting outside on a balcony overlooking the ocean in a rather stiff wind in the so-called smoking section of the restaurant. The anti-smoking crusader almost stabbed me with his salad fork. After all, America is a free country. Here's the script:

MAN [*from behind me*]: Please put that pipe out.

I pretend not to have heard him.

MAN: Put that damn pipe out.

ME: Are you talking to me?

MAN: Put that God-damn pipe away.

ME: Where do you want me to put it?

MAN: Up your arse.

ME: This is a rather expensive pipe. A Dunhill. Do you know how much they cost?

MAN: I'm getting really angry.

ME: You should try pipe smoking ... keeps you cool.

MAN: You fucking arsehole.

He runs off and returns with the cook. By now the Man is out of his mind. Is, I suspect, 'high' on something.

COOK: Would you please put your pipe away, sir?

ME: No, I won't.

COOK: Please, sir.

ME: No.
COOK: We can find you another table.
ME: No.
COOK: Why not?
ME: This is a smoking section.
COOK: Yes, but no pipes.
ME: Where does it say: 'No pipes'?
COOK: That's the rule.
ME: Whose rule?
COOK: We don't allow pipe smoking in our restaurant.
ME: Why not?
MAN: Because it stinks.
ME: [to the man] You're starting to bother me.
He tries to grab my pipe and with his salad fork pushes me against the balcony. The Cook pulls him back.
ME: Call the police.
COOK: Come on, gentlemen, let's be sensible.
ME: Good idea.
MAN: That guy is fucked.
The Cook whispers to the Man. He gestures wildly. A waitress arrives and helps him to remove his plate and wine bottle to another table. His mouse of a woman looks at me with intense hatred. Order returns. I re-light me pipe and walk away from my table, from this insanity.

Near the beach is a stand with bicycles for hire. I decide to take a bike and ride along the beach. After all, it is a nice day. The bicycle man looks at me. Refuses my money.
ME: What's the matter?
BICYCLE MAN: This is a non-smoking bicycle.
ME: What do you mean?
BICYCLE MAN: You can't smoke on this bicycle.
ME: [stunned] You can't be serious.

> *He points to a sign. 'Bicycles for hire. No smoking.' I re-light my pipe, wish him a 'nice day' and take a long walk along the ocean black with oil and plastic wastage.*

And here is another amazing story.

I once walked into a supermarket in Los Angeles and was greeted by a large sign that read 'Shampoo Week'. My curiosity got the better of me and a charming blonde guided me towards a mysterious treasure island at the back of the store. Big signs of welcome: 'This is Shampoo Week'. At every corner a magnetic field made my hair stand up on my head. Mirrors were strategically placed to reflect this humiliation. I started to grow a little uneasy, but my guide and companion assured me that there was nothing to worry about. Of course, her hair stayed in perfect shape. Suddenly — lights and action! We had arrived at a large, bubbling display. Shampoo for normal hair, abnormal hair, shampoo for dry hair (what is dry hair actually?) shampoo for pubic hair, young hair, old hair, no hair, dark hair, light hair and then there was 'curly, soft hair'.

The girl by my side asked me what shampoo I used and tenderly brushed my hair off my forehead. I thought of my mother and helplessly fondled a large bottle in front of me.

> ME: Sometimes I use baby shampoo.
> GIRL: What type?
> ME: I have no idea.
> GIRL: What type of conditioner?
> ME: I never use conditioner.

She frowned. My last bit of courage evaporated. She called upon a large, middle-aged creature in white. The Shampoo Matron! I recognised my school teacher in first grade and wanted to throw myself at her bosom. 'Forgive me and hold me. I didn't mean to ...'

She was most distressed. Here was a person who used baby shampoo and no conditioner.

'Can I ask you a few questions?', she said.

I felt dizzy, overwhelmed by guilt, needing to sit down. Then I found myself in a darkish room with the matron carefully examining my 'split ends'. I had always thought this to be some pop group, but how wrong one can be. I confessed everything: that my mother had used Sunlight Soap for years after the war, that I had occasionally used washing powder and that I usually cut my hair in the mirror with ordinary scissors. From her distraught face, I realised I had reached rock bottom. Everything I had done was wrong. Totally wrong. My hair could fall out at any moment.

Beneath her efficient front, however, was a tender human soul at work. I was given a large bag of free samples, brochures, pamphlets, useful hints and an assurance that everything would come good in the end. All was not lost.

After this hair-raising experience, I found myself walking the empty streets of Los Angeles, clutching my bag of goodies, wondering how many shampoos were not biodegradable, what effects their conditioners and hair spray were having on the ozone layer and how our good earth copes with conditioner. Shampoo is probably one of our less harmful indulgences. But those shiny bubbles are slowly choking us ...

The West is so preoccupied with consumerism that peace and happiness can apparently only be achieved through wealth. Recently I heard on the news that Australia's falling birthrate could jeopardise its economic future ...

Anyone who is afraid of the future, especially a so-called economic future, has no future. I feel it is only when we can put one leg in the East and the other in the West that some solution can be found and that we can give the good and the bad on either side our loving understanding.

Nothing earns respect more quickly than to be a greedy consumer. With modesty and consideration you get nowhere. Words like tenderness and gentleness have almost disappeared from our vocabulary. We've become dependent on our ability to consume. What is necessary today is an exile from materialism and rampant technology. But that is not easy — we all indulge in it. There's a great need for simplicity. Only then can we find something infinitely greater than our earthbound complexities. We only have to look at the ocean. What a mighty god, perhaps too much for us, but what an inspiration and indication of what lies beyond man.

I love making films and I've been fortunate enough to get away with the type of films I've wanted to make. I have always believed that people are basically starving to see a bit of humanity on the screen. One must never underestimate the public. I get deeply upset when I see films made by committees who think they know what the public is looking for, when I know that people want something that touches them. But say this to one of those creative producers in Hollywood and he'll say: 'What do you mean, what emotional truths? This is show business, man. We need to hook them.' 'That's entertainment!' is one of the most arrogant sayings on earth. What's entertaining to some, can be extremely boring to others.

I think it was Andrei Tarkovsky who remarked that if film is art, why do people expect it to be easily understood? Nobody expects this from the other arts. Most films I see take me away from the heart of humanity. I like to believe that life must be an act of love, and despite all the disappointments, I still fervently love people. I'm interested in people, not only for what they say and how they behave; I'm interested in their silences.

In films the 'inner' rarely comes to the surface, yet film is the very medium that can penetrate and then project one's inner side. The most obvious problem is that film has become larger than life; leaving no room for life's realities. That's why I don't like 'stars' who project larger-than-life characters. Each thinking, feeling, struggling individual is much bigger than any of them.

What a paradox to work in a medium filled with all these contradictions. It's the most wonderful invention of our century. Unfortunately mostly misused and abused. Peter Watkins, one of the most talented and versatile film directors in the world, has for many years protested against the abuse and misuse of the medium. His willingness to speak up and force debate has cost him dearly. A filmmaker of great integrity — shunned and mistrusted by those who hold the purse-strings — lost to a profession that needs people like him desperately. In his paper of 1997, 'The Dark Side of the Moon' he writes:

> Today, seventy years after the Hollywood cinema began to make its huge impact on society, we still have no tradition of discussing, critically, how the audio-visual media affect us. In the early days, human interactivity on many levels had a real and meaningful part in the functioning of society. We continued to use time and interactive human process of these activities and that's helped to counter and diffuse the more manipulative effects of the early cinema. There was a balance. But the advent of television radically and swiftly changed all that, by adopting and adapting the most authoritarian aspects of the cinema's language, form and narrative structures, and imposing them on a global society via a largely undebated, unchallenged saturation coverage which is little short of breathtaking in its speed, its arrogance and its secrecy.

I have no doubt that had television taken an alternative direction and worked in a more open and complex way with the public, global society today would be vastly more humane and just.

I'm glad I never had much success until I was forty. It made me tough enough to stay on the pathway I'd chosen. Despite the many obstacles and with the help of my friends, I proceeded to make my own films. Besides, what is success? It's not dictated by the outside world. Success is only within oneself and can only be judged by each one of us separately.

Why it had to be such a battleground I still find hard to understand. After all I meant no harm! 'Keep on recording the vultures, even if they're feasting on our own bones', wrote a friend. I believe in the individual. I believe in the intelligence of audiences, in people's capacity to feel. I've always had great respect for the audience. Wherever I introduce my films the inevitable question comes up: 'For whom do you actually make your films?' I always say: 'For you and for you and for you etc.' pointing at individual people — then — 'But not for the lot of you.'

Departing words from an enthusiastic producer/con man in Hollywood:
'I'm passionately committed to your project.'
Never heard from him again.

American distributor who failed to honour a verbal contract:
'Beautiful film ... I loved it ... Unfortunately it's not for us our company would never do it justice.'

Producer at Cannes flicking through the pages of a new brochure:
'Where are the tits, George? Where the hell are the tits?'

Hollywood agent ready to sign me up:
'I'm not a high concept guy. I'm a unique individual in this business.'

Parting words from a distributor who refused to pay us our share: 'We'll communicate long distance ...'
Same man:
- It's true ... I must be honest with you ...Your film did quite well but, as you know, we had some horrendous expenses. It'll take some time before we see any money.
- You mean, before I see any money?
- Yeah, that's right.
- What about the money you've made already?
- We're in this together — you know that.

Conversation with a female producer in Venice, wearing a purple hat and matching handbag:
- How much did your film *Island* cost?'
- What do you think?'
- I guess about six or seven ... oh, no, maybe that's too much ... I know you work with low budgets ... probably five ...'
- No ... one million.'
- No ... no ... not what you got paid ... the budget ... what was the budget?
- One million.
- Why can't you tell me?
- Obviously I can't.

Admiring female:
- I loved your film *Local Hero* ...
- That wasn't my film. That was Bill ...
- You don't have to be so modest. I love your work.

Hollywood producer:
- Here's a script my wife wrote... She wants you to do it.
- What's the story?

- It's the greatest load of bull you've ever read. Please tell her you're impressed, but too busy.

And another producer in Hollywood:
- Here, have a look at this.
- What is it?
- My wife's. She's written the script. It's absolutely marvellous.
- What's the story?
- I'll be damned ... shit ... I couldn't tell you.

Boss of a television station after having seen one of my films. He's standing next to me in the men's, talking to his offsider behind him:
OFFSIDER: What did you think of Paul Cox's film?
BOSS: What a heap of shit. He's the biggest wanker in the business
ME: I thought it was great.
Pause.
BOSS: You don't know your arse from your fellow, old boy.
ME: I am Paul Cox.
Long pause.
BOSS: Sorry!

Very famous American actress:
- I love all your films.
- Which one have you seen?
- I haven't seen any, but my friends — the ones I trust — just love them.

Angry union rep:
- I know about your type of films.
- What do you mean?

- You know damn well what I mean.
- No, I don't.
- Don't play funny buggers with me, my friend. I don't like your type of films.
- What type of films?
- I think I've made my point.

In Toronto I had dinner with a producer who had just spent millions on a film condemned by the critics and ignored by the masses. He and his 'creative team' had tried hard to please everyone. I asked him why this film was still being screened all over the world.

He said: 'Don't you understand, we are losing a lot of money?' I found this rather arrogant and told him so.

Why should a shocking movie like that have to bore me in the plane, be shown on cable in every hotel room and find its way in cinemas around the world? What gives one country the right to exhibit a bad movie all over the world 'because we are losing money', when most local product can't even find an exhibitor or is removed from the local cinema as soon as the next blockbuster arrives. In order to attract audiences there has been a growing reliance on graphic violence of all kinds in these blockbusters. It's absurd to say that violence on the screen has no effect on the public. Let me quote you a few examples from an article I found in the *New York Times*.

> Nathanial White recently ripped a woman open with a knife, slitting her from the top of her chest to her abdomen. He told the police he saw it done in the movie *Robocop I* and *Robocop II* dozens of times.
>
> In Salt Lake City, Utah, William Andrews was executed by lethal injection ... for a killing he said he copied from the Clint Eastwood 1973 movie *Magnum Force*. During a hold-

up at a hi-fi store, Andrews and a friend forced five hostages to drink drain cleaner, Drano. All but one died.

A nine-year-old girl was sexually assaulted with a broom handle by four other children on a deserted beach in San Francisco. They said they copied it from the Linda Blair prison movie *Born Innocent* they had seen on TV.

These are just a few of the more prominent cases. Some years ago *Silence of the Lambs* won the Academy Award for best picture. That was indeed a grim moment for any thinking, struggling filmmaker. A serial killer fond of human liver plays cat and mouse with a female investigator and in the end walks free to make a sequel possible. Yes, the film was well made and well acted and well directed, but so was the Second World War.

Once a year Telluride, a small township in the heart of Colorado, hosts a prestigious film festival, or rather a film weekend, where film buffs meet to celebrate the latest 'serious movies'. I was honoured once with a small retrospective, and a few years later, together with Isabelle Huppert, was asked to return with our film *Cactus*. Before the screening I was to introduce Isabelle, who this time was the guest of honour.

Telluride is an extremely beautiful spot in the mountains. In the afternoon before our screening, Isabelle and I drove into the country, sat quietly near a mountain stream and listened to the wonderful sounds around us. I have a very clear recollection of the light that played on the water. Much depends on the nature of light.

We peacefully made our way back to town and arrived early enough to attend the first screening of Andrei Tarkovsky's *The Sacrifice*. I knew of Tarkovsky's problems in trying to get the film off the ground. No American producer would touch him and it is to the great credit of the Swedish Film Institute that he was finally allowed to make this film with their help in Sweden.

Tarkovsky was a rare and noble being and certainly one of the finest filmmakers ever. *The Sacrifice* moved me very deeply. On the way back to the hotel, I had to stop the car to collect myself.

There was an hour left before our premiere and instead of rehearsing my little speech to introduce Isabelle — this was her evening, a celebration of her career — I found myself furiously writing a speech against the American film industry. I don't know what got into me. I knew of Tarkovsky's fatal illness, how difficult it was for him to survive as a filmmaker and how much he'd fought to retain his integrity. My ill-timed, badly prepared speech ran as follows:

> Thank you for inviting *Cactus* to Telluride and for paying this tribute to Isabelle Huppert. I can't think of anyone who deserves it more, especially here where people, for a few days at least, are serious about film. So far I haven't heard the word 'product' once and even the question, "What's your next project?" hasn't been asked.
>
> Unfortunately I have to digress a little here, as I've just seen the real sacrifice Andrei Tarkovsky made with his film *The Sacrifice*. From the town of Larissa in Greece to the city of Arles in France, I've recently seen Rocky fighting for his tenth title, Rambo committing more obscenities and Arnold Schwarzenegger terminating anything that moved around him. Today I saw an extraordinary film made by an extraordinarily courageous man. No American producer or company wanted to help him make the film, yet you're all here now celebrating his sacrifice. It must be embarrassing for any thinking, feeling American to find even the smallest cinema in Europe loaded with films like, *Teen Werewolf*, *The Karate Kid* or *Top Gun* representing your country, together with McDonalds and Kentucky Fried, while you could have been the proud producer of this important contribution to contemporary cinema.
>
> Walking the streets of Manhattan is a far more exciting experience than watching the average American movie. Why

is this in a country that harbours the amazing Julliard School of Music, has the finest dance and opera companies and a bubbling cultural life that embraces many cultures? Why all this wonderful activity can't rub off a little on your cinema, is an appalling mystery. Cinema in this country is nothing but the manufacture of bad taste, which is pretty tricky stuff when you realise that the right marketing of chicken wings or hamburgers can change the form and shape of less advanced countries.

Film wasn't invented to patronise and corrupt our children and to appeal mostly to our lower instincts. America is the country that has the power to change the future use of the medium, to restore some balance, to allow people like Tarkovsky to speak. After all you control, legally or illegally, most screens around the world and could bring love and peace and true imagination to those screens, instead of constant exploitation. I know of many marvellously talented people in your country who, in this climate of exploitation, will never get a chance to show what this country really has to offer.

I'm not totally condemning what most of you think is 'the right stuff', but I'm pleading for some balance. I'm asking you to restore the cinema to its true potential and once again make it available to grown-ups.

We live in difficult and extremely dangerous times. Man has no history of being able to handle power. Power has always been abused and misused. We all know the power of the media. Film, of all media, could help us to see again, to feel again, to love again. The Third Reich used film very successfully. Goebbels was fully aware of its potential. Let's all thank the gods that television hadn't been invented then. If Hitler and Goebbels had been able to go on daily talk-back shows, the Third Reich would probably still be marching.

I did see *Top Gun* and was appalled. Its budget was at least thirty times more than that of *The Sacrifice*. To think that *Top Gun* will be seen by a hundred million people and *The Sacrifice* by a handful, is horrifying.

I'm here to introduce Isabelle Huppert and I'm sorry I

had to digress. I just wonder what would have happened to Isabelle had she been born and raised in America and *The Lacemaker* had been a 'package' aimed at a particular youth market. Most probably the film would never have been made or, if by some fluke the film had gone through the system, it would never have had the same poignant integrity. Too many experts would have stood by to tell the director Claude Goretta how to make it more marketable.

Isabelle never neglected the inner, always gave the characters she portrayed a true dimension. A unique talent quietly blossomed on the other side of the Atlantic in an atmosphere that still recognises film as a means of self-expression. She has become one of the finest actresses of our time. She's now ready for Hollywood and by God, Hollywood needs her!

I've somehow reconstructed this speech from the bits and pieces I later found in my pockets. There was, of course, no applause and much disapproval. When my name appeared on the screen, the audience was not impressed. The next day I was more or less ignored and left Telluride in a state of deep depression.

Five years later I was invited to return to Telluride, which gave me the chance to apologise. I did. Not for what I had said, but for the tactlessness of my timing. This time I shared a platform with one of the last great poets of the cinema — Krzysztof Kieslowski. A woman came to give me a hug and thank me for *A Woman's Tale*. When she'd gone Kieslowski asked:

'Who's she?'

'That's Jodi Foster.'

'Don't know her,' he said.

Dreams, Stories and Magic Moments

Every film starts with a small magic moment — mostly only recognised years after the event. A word, a smile, or an image attaches itself to the subconscious and will not let go. Sometimes these illuminations have an immediate impact. To prevent them haunting me, I write them down.

The following reflections have been interwoven, in one form or another, into my films —- or will probably emerge somewhere in the future.

Dolphins
The child in us must never die. Our richest moments are those moments when we observe the world like a child, liberated from time, place and rationality. Society does its utmost to destroy the child in us and the consumer society kills it. Every time a camera is being set up, I wait impatiently like a child for the moment I can

look through the camera, It's always the first time. It can bring such excitement that focusing and aperture control become irrelevant.

When I first crossed the ocean I saw a school of dolphins rising above the waves, dancing on the waves. They played around the boat for some time. Every time they emerged, I felt a great flash of excitement. What glory, what magic! The memory of that image and my response to it, has travelled with me ever since. It's only when I see trained dolphins trapped in an enclosure that this 'illumination' becomes obscured.

When I see a picture of slaughtered dolphins, I go into a state of shock. Feel a deep sense of hurt and loss. The child in me is threatened and ready to die. Yesterday I heard that some deep-sea dolphins had tried to commit suicide on a South Australian beach. Some succeeded, others were rescued. I had never heard of 'deep-sea dolphins'. I'd seen 'ordinary dolphins' rising from the waves, but now I try to follow their brothers in that vast darkness of the seas. How deep do they travel? I follow them and see them gliding through those darker layers, those darker depths. Now the image of the dancing dolphin has an inner image, a brother who travels in the deep — a subconscious shadow that makes the image of the dancing dolphin even more glorious, more complete. In the midst of all this, man's endeavours remain on the surface. They seem so trivial, so tragically out of tune.

Auvers-sur-Oise
The little town where Vincent van Gogh spent the last few months. I walk past the church that he painted so vigorously. The rain has stopped. Where did he sit or stand to paint this church? I find my way up to the cemetery. The sun burns through the clouds now. A lark begins to sing. I've never heard a lark sing so loudly. I visualise Vincent's funeral, remember Emile Bernard's exclamation: 'What a deplorable day for us artists.'

I have no trouble finding Vincent's grave. Together with his brother he lies peacefully against the wall of the cemetery.

Ici repose Vincent van Gogh
Ici repose Theodore van Gogh

I cut a leaf from the ivy that grows over and unites both graves. The lark is now right above my head. I sit down and weep. Later in the Maison de van Gogh, I imagine Vincent's body laid out amidst the flowers — masses of flowers; the sunflowers he loved so much, yellow dahlias, yellow, yellow flowers everywhere. Bernard said it was his favourite colour — symbol of the light that burnt in his heart. On the walls, all his last canvases, forming something like a halo around him. A passing peasant who joined the mourners whispered: 'Vincent painted the sun.'

I go up to his room on the second floor. Did you really die here, in this tiny little room on that rusty old bed, dear Vincent? I lie down on his bed, turn to the wall, look up through the narrow window above. 'I wish I could go home now', he said quietly to his brother before he died.

Someone comes up the stairs. I jump up and try to hide behind the door. A woman enters. She turns to her companion outside and whispers: *'C'est triste, n'est-ce pas? Très triste'*.

A meeting in New York
She was sixty-one, she told me, and grotesque. Maybe twenty stone or more. She breathed with difficulty and just managed to move around the room. Her companion, a little poodle, nervously kept jumping up on her enormous bosom to lick her face. She was highly articulate, spoke many languages, was slightly psychic. Her immense loneliness had distorted the shape of her face and body. People laugh at these creatures; children throw stones; Fellini used to put them into his movies.

After much vodka and laughter, I departed and kissed her goodbye. I tried to kiss her on the cheek, but she turned her face

'What a deplorable day for us artists.'

and my kiss landed on her lips and with it came centuries of love and lust, flesh and blood. Of longing, tenderness and hope. Her tears came from behind the iron curtain, from inside the concentration camps, from the heart of all wars being fought, from the very heart of human consciousness. Her parting embrace had unexpected lust. My ignorance cut like a sharp knife through my veins. 'I'm just another Jew', she said as the door closed between us.

A railway station in Eastern Europe
The train came to a sudden halt. We'd been ushered into this barren restaurant and asked to wait. Now I can see my fellow travellers. Not a happy lot, I must say.

Near the window in the sun, a large fat man is drinking beer. The woman at his side has such a lined face that I can hardly see her eyes. She too, drinks beer, large pots of beer. The man's face is red with thick, purple veins. More beer, a schnapps, another schnapps. He abuses the waiter, walks past me and urinates loudly in the toilet block next door. I can hear him spitting, coughing and farting.

He comes back a new man. Staggers to his table. More drinks. They've started to argue. The argument is about the waiter, who refuses to argue with them. The man forces a large sausage into his mouth and with his finger scrapes some mustard from his plate. He licks his finger like a child. More beer; soon he will explode.

The station-master enters: 'All on board, please.' The woman helps the man onto the train. I make sure I don't get on until the couple have settled, then desperately hope that my carriage will be left behind.

Hotels in foreign cities
Walls either empty or decorated with prints by a would-be artist who knew the manager. Mini-bars that glare at you and gently open their doors at the slightest touch. Television sets which blare the same nonsense from room to room. Maids who come and 'turn

your bed' for the night. Air conditioners without a switch. Cold, inhuman air on sultry summer nights. Distant traffic noises, drunken voices coming out of lifts. Laughter from pleased business men as they celebrate their day. Phone calls to the world — anyone, anywhere, anytime. Muzak from hidden speakers. Can I please go home?

A visit to Auschwitz
Arbeit macht frei — the gates of hell. The gates of death. *Arbeit macht frei*. The rain falls, the wind cries, clouds drift by. Soldiers march through that black gate in my heart. *Arbeit macht frei*. A small bird calls loudly, too loudly. Another bird answers.

We enter the barracks with the shoes and the bones and the hair and the suitcases full of horror. *Arbeit macht frei*. The courtyard for the special executions. Here's the spot where they stood. Where they died. Flowers decorate the lead wall behind. I stand on that patch of soil. Stare at the vast greyness, the naked trees, the empty sky. *Arbeit macht frei*.

A bullet pierces my forehead, blood spills everywhere. Suddenly I feel my daughter's hand in mine. A tearful face. 'I'm so sad, Daddy. Let's please go home.'

Night in Greece
Night away from home. Night at home. Night in Greece. A red moon hangs low. Ancient ruins drip with blood — our blood, your blood, my blood. The sea, a dark blue mirror dotted with stars. In the far distance, a boat struggling against the tide. The figure of a lonely captain stands tall and strong on deck. He's in charge of the sea. I remember a melody — a song from Crete. Heard it on my way home some five hundred years ago.

A fresh spring morning
A fresh spring morning with new flowers and shy, white butterflies. Your name hangs in the air like a passing cloud ... lingering. People, whole armies of people, march through the skies. The sun lies

stretched out across the universe like an enormous mother on fire. I become a fish, a crocodile, a bird. My feathers feed a young tree. I travel into a new leaf, into a flower. Glide along with its fragrance back into the soil, return to the earth. Become a worm, a rat, a creature of the dark, die a thousand deaths. Then slowly turn to stone.

The rock breaks and I find myself inside your womb — a tiny cell that gathers arms and legs. As I emerge from your body we embrace with such tenderness that the universe shudders.

'I love you,' she whispers
An ancient woman in a wheelchair calls me over. There are many people standing around, drinking, talking. They leave her alone. I kneel down and kiss her hand. Her movements are jerky, almost mechanical. She seems in great pain. She wants to speak and I lower my ear to her mouth, but feel her lips curling around my ear and her tongue awkwardly finding a way inside. I press my lips against hers. Her lips are warm and passionate, despite the hard cracks in her skin. My hand slips down her dress — did she force it down? I feel her chest — old, hard, stony nipples with no flesh. Suddenly her breasts start to grow in my hand. Her mouth soft and mellow, kissing me with great tenderness. As I open my eyes I see her face slowly growing younger, then changing into a woman of great beauty. My hands merge with her flesh. 'I love you', she whispers as I disappear into the darkness of her immense body.

A dream in the plane from Tokyo to Moscow
A Roman city with a busy square. I'm about twelve years old, dressed in a white robe and dark hair-band. Someone ushers me towards a staircase, leading towards a temple above the square. Behind me, the pillars of the surrounding walls. I start to climb the steps and, as I ascend, I feel my body growing older. At every landing I have to take a rest and reassess the situation. The higher I climb, the more respect the people pay me.

Finally I arrive at the top, a very old man. A large chair is waiting for me, a kind of throne. I sit down and look out over the city. The people down below are waving at me; some are shouting, raising their fists. I have great trouble standing up. I try to move away from the throne, but an invisible force holds me back. I know death is very close. I can feel my life ebbing. An ancient woman comes to my rescue. My mother? She helps me to move away from the throne. I know that if I manage from this point to take one step forward, I will regain my youth, keep my life. But I will lose my power, my authority. The old woman helps me, encourages me. I get to the steps, almost fall down. As soon as I go down a step, the woman disappears, dissolves, and some power returns to my body. At the same time, I feel a tremendous loss. When I finally arrive at the bottom I am a young boy again and my body and spirit merge with the people.

**ptt *A dream during a short siesta in Israel* **

A pregnant woman leans against a broken fence. A strong wind blows her hair across her face. She's surrounded by black birds that fly without moving their wings. Suddenly the cobblestones of my youth, with a wild horse galloping up and down the main street. The houses are in ruins, still smoking. This street is a short cut from the railway station to my parents' house. I pass the church with no steeple. Monks are carrying heavy stones towards a burning altar. Our street is still there with the houses in good order, but the cobblestones have changed. The street is now a large mirror reflecting the sky, the sea, the universe. Every step I take leaves a dark footprint out of which a tree emerges. A forest grows behind me. A large, thick forest full of mysteries.

I arrive at the house of my youth. A pale moon hovers above. My mother is at the door, waiting with her soft embrace. Suddenly the mirror becomes water. We start to drown. The horse returns, galloping in great panic through the drowning forest. It gallops into a tree. I see the horn of a unicorn piercing the bark. The tree starts to bleed. Now the whole drowning forest bleeds. We're standing in a sea of blood. The mirror can still be seen, reflecting the fading cobblestones of my youth.

A dream in Toronto

We are shooting a small film somewhere with a very large crew. There are people everywhere. Some of them I seem to know. Others are total strangers. They speak a language I don't understand. Gaffers and grips have built large structures for no apparent purpose. The set is enormous with cranes and dollies travelling at random in front of me. It's a bewildering experience. Norman Kaye and Wendy Hughes seem to be the protagonists, but I also spot Gosia Dobrowolska and Hugo Weaving together with a large man in a fur coat. Norman is close to the end of a long speech, but suddenly he indicates that he can't remember his last three lines. He requests a crane to lift him up to the ceiling where he starts to look for his lost lines.

Wendy screams from down below not to be so stupid. 'His lost lines are on the floor.'

I call: '*Action!*' but nothing happens. A journalist walks onto the set and although she is told I'm busy, insists on talking to me. She is doing an article on an exhibition of her words and my paintings. I ask her how she got hold of my paintings, but she ignores me.

I'm being forced into a room with a large, open fireplace, old chairs and heavy paintings and ornaments. A fire is burning in front of the fireplace and has already burned a hole in the carpet and the floor. John Larkin appears. This is his room. He argues that a fire outside the fireplace heats the room better than a fire inside the fireplace!

I say: 'What about the floor and the smoke?'. I can hardly see John, who insists there is no smoke. The journalist has lifted a picture off the wall and finds a poem that upsets her because her name is not mentioned. It's written on bits of paper stuck to the wall. I suddenly realise that there is a camera running at 64 frames per second. I scream out, but the camera runs even faster.

Norman is now carried on a stretcher up a newly built staircase. He screams at me: 'Get off the set. I am acting.' I ask Paul Ammitzboll to help me stop the camera, but he can't do anything about it either.

We're called outside to watch a soccer game, but there are no players. Everyone is totally engrossed watching the empty field. Now and then someone disappears or falls down. Ambulance attendants carry the bodies off. Peter Watkins stands next to me and explains that we are watching the game of life.

'People are so preoccupied with the game that they don't notice when their neighbour dies,' he says.

Meanwhile, someone tells me that there is a woman in the cellar down below who insists on talking to me. She threatens to disrupt the film if she is not allowed on the set.

Gosia goes downstairs, now dressed in red, and returns looking extremely angry. 'This woman is mad,' she says, 'doesn't want to leave. Her name is Alice Walker.' I have no idea who Alice Walker is. She claims to have properties all over the world, including 'Talm Beach'.

Gosia says: 'If she doesn't know that it is Palm Beach, she is a fake.'

Suddenly a hand with enormous fingernails at least ten centimetres long digs through the floor and starts to rearrange small items left behind. I grab the camera and film the hand in tight close up. The place is now empty. Only the long fingernails are left, tapping on the wooden planks.

The death of a father

A friend from Jerusalem phones and tells me about her husband's death and how she misses his hand and touch at night. Her voice, soft and hurt. Alone. I put the phone down, feel deeply for her loss.

The phone rings again. My brother's voice from Germany. '*Papa is dood.*' Our father died … He died last night. We couldn't reach you …' My brother's voice breaks. I talk. We cry. We disconnect.

I sit for hours staring at the fading light. When my daughter comes home, we weep together. Alone, outside in the garden, I scream long and hard. Two doves take flight and a bell rings from afar. Inside my head the chaos goes on. Why didn't you once, only once, hold my head, just once touch my face, dear Father? Your heart was so black, so lost. Your pain spread so far.

I can't go the funeral. I can't.

Two months later we stand at his graveside. He lies next to my mother in a small patch of soil under some fine old trees. My mother has been lying here for eight years. Her body must have withered. Her body has gone … I imagine the holes in her skull in which the most loving eyes once lived. My parents were separated in life and now lie together.

My daughter rearranges the flowers. My sister fetches water. The others weep. I walk away from the grave into a clutter of gravestones, towards a long row of pines. What a beautiful place this is, the only part of this town that has kept its peace and grown more beautiful. That 'great grief of mankind' suddenly becomes too much. Dear me.

I wander further into the graveyard and feel only pain and tears and hopelessness. An old woman in black is polishing a gravestone. Meticulously she sprays the wax and meticulously she polishes that cold, black marble. Then stands back to check the shine and the reflections of the light. She turns around, looks at me. I'm an intruder, an outsider, a witness to her most intimate moment. Her mournful eyes fill with suspicion — fear — hatred. My tears give her no comfort. A bird starts to sing. I've never heard a bird sing so beautifully.

I return to my father's grave. I've come here to make peace, to forget, to forgive. 'It wasn't your fault, dear Father, it wasn't anybody's fault.'

My daughter grabs my hand. Dear, sweet little woman. She knows. She understands.

Niagara Falls

Maybe we're limited by the beliefs and traditions we inherit from our ancestors, I don't know. But when tradition and belief are in the hands of politicians and developers who worship progress at any cost, our basic sense of reality disappears. We enter a strange Luna Park of greed which in the end reduces the family home to a piece of real estate and replaces the family watch with the 'swatch'.

Our home, the earth, suffers deeply. Mankind becomes totally out of tune with nature and consequently out of tune with himself. Most of our cities alienate the people and the loneliness and unhappiness of the people who 'have everything' is much larger than we are allowed to believe. The consumer society must celebrate the 'outer' at all costs and even extraordinary power manifestations in nature like the Niagara Falls — in the past worshipped like a god — have to be exploited to the last drop.

In our hire car we drove into a township spotted with cheap motels. This didn't correspond at all with the vivid memories we had exchanged on our journey. Memories of photographs and stories from our respective youths. We expected a rain forest out of which this power manifestation of nature would flow.

The noise of the falls was awesome but the noise of the little tourist planes soon destroyed the purity of that sound. Thousands of people were hanging around the falls with their photo and video cameras. Down below, where the water had come to rest again, a large substance of thick, green froth. 'A minor pollution problem'! There were little boats struggling upstream, filled with tourists in hired plastic Ku-Klux-Klan outfits to weather the storm. In despair we ran to the top and managed to work our way through the crowd, to the water's edge. Suddenly we saw the river actually breathing like a colossal, living thing. Right in front of us the water gathered speed and then became fire, sky, earth then water again. This was the moment of conception, the moment of birth, the moment of death.

How strangely out of tune we are with this force. I don't know why, but I remembered the soft singing of my mother at night when I, as a small child, lingering on the threshold of sleep, could feel her goodnight kiss lovingly become part of my dreams.

We saw no ugliness on the way down to town; nothing enraged us any longer. That thundering edge of eternal sleep had soothed all the pain, all discomfort within. We'd slipped over the edge and felt complete. This experience became 'a glimpse of reality' in the film *A Woman's Tale*. The waterfall gave a crucial metaphor to the 'universal death' of the main character.

South Africa

I'd never been to this country. Apartheid was one of the most bizarre and humiliating aberrations of the human mind. Now I've been invited to the Cape Town Film Festival with a small retrospective — part of the celebration of South Africa's first year of democracy. Our film *Exile*, the film I can't get released in my own country, is opening the festival.

In Johannesburg I'm cheerfully received by three customs officials who speak a language I almost understand. My Dutch makes them laugh, one in particular. He's a large man with a large tooth sticking out of large lips. His tonsils dance wildly in the back of his mouth. Not a pretty sight. I explain why I've come and what I do. He's not impressed. The tonsils close up, the lips retract. The tooth becomes a fang, ready to attack. The youngest of the three helps me on my way to Cape Town. 'Sorry about the boss, welcome to South Africa', he says. Did I miss something?

There's no official engagement on the first day, so I'm taken on a trip along the narrow ocean road towards the Cape. As we pause to watch a magnificent sunset, a small Toyota sedan parks near by. In the front a smart black couple and in the back I count eight smiling faces. They pour out of the Toyota and dance around. Oh what a feeling!

The next morning on the television three vignettes about last year's voting. An old couple enter the polling station holding hands. They're told to go to separate booths to vote. The man refuses. What's the matter? We've been together for sixty years, she's my wife, we've never been separated. He refuses to leave her side. Next an old soldier, known for many years as the village fool, digs up his old war medals and marches through the township like a black Charles de Gaulle, saluting the bewildered bystanders on his way to the polling booths. Then a woman who's been waiting for two days in a queue to cast her vote, is asked why she isn't complaining. 'I've been waiting for forty years for this. What's another day?'

Exile is warmly received. When the village priest (played by Chris Haywood) staring across the waters to the distant island of the exile says: 'On a clear day I can see enough of that island to make me feel ashamed', some people applaud. The next day I realise. On a clear day from the shores of Cape Town you can see Robben Island. This is where Nelson Mandela spent twenty-seven years of his life. He now stands next to his jailers, with a forgiveness that restores one's faith in the human race. Everyone speaks highly of Mandela. I think quite a few of our world leaders should spend twenty-seven years in jail before proceeding with their task.

A remarkable collection of people have been invited to a lunch at the Australian High Commission. They all manage to laugh about the past — even the brooding black poet who was jailed for many years and badly tortured. He now has a position in the government. On the way back, the director of the festival tells me more about this courageous man and about his own time on death row when he tried to smuggle someone out of the country. The agony of the past is delivered so casually.

The next day is Independence Day. People seem unanimously surprised about their new South Africa but are divided about what has been achieved and recognise that this could still turn into civil war. Yet in the town square thousands have gathered to sing and dance and celebrate. That night a small group of black people is standing outside my window. They are chanting, singing ... Now and then someone screams. A long, primal scream full of agony.

Over dinner everyone takes his and her turn to cry and laugh. Emotions run high. Later, much later, back in my room, I hear a mother singing to her child, I hear the sea pounding the shore, I hear distant drums echo through the night and I travel back through time and space into the heart of Africa.

The next morning a small van takes me into a few of the many large shanty towns surrounding Cape Town. Our black guide and protector assures me that at least two million blacks live here. There's a broken spirit here; conditions are appalling. An angry, drunken man confronts and threatens me. I realise if he gets support we could be in trouble.

More out of fear than cheek, I say: 'Don't give me any of that black and white stuff — my blood is the same colour as yours'. His friends laugh and usher him away. Our guide swiftly moves us back into the van. I think we're lucky.

I meet some wonderful young people at the master class for media students. I ask them which films they've seen and what films they like. The only film most of them have seen is *Pulp Fiction*. Oh dear ... They start to talk about their own lives, their own pasts, and how apartheid has affected their lives. How many people in their direct environment were killed or disappeared altogether. There are real stories to be told here. Meanwhile, at the window, a large black woman is cleaning the glass meticulously. Now and then she pushes her face against the window and stares at us all with large, curious eyes. She is the mother of all mothers. This is no pulp fiction. She is real. Her presence precipitates a passionate explosion from the students of their own truths. They realise that their own stories have to be filmed. The picture that will always remain with me from this highly-charged confrontation is of the bus driving away, the students with their arms out of the windows, fists clenched, singing loudly: '*Viva!*'

On the way back in the plane I sit next to a South African engineer. He is coming to Australia to establish a new life. He tells me gruesome stories about people being murdered in front of his house and how Johannesburg has turned into a war zone. He assures me it was much better during apartheid. I'm too exhausted to argue. I wish him good luck and fall into a deep sleep.

To catch a plane

I am driving my friend in a hurry to catch a plane. It is busy on the freeway, too busy.

'We are not going to make it', my friend whispers.

'Yes, we will, you just wait.' I bring the car to a grinding halt in front of the wrong terminal. 'Never mind, we have plenty of time. Come on.' Indeed, we make it.

I proudly wave at her and return to my car. What car? My car is gone, towed away, stolen, cut to pieces. I run across the road and ask a taxi driver:

'Did you see anyone driving an old white station wagon?'.

'No, mate, sorry.'

There are three chauffeurs standing next to their limousines. They must have seen my car taking off with the wrong driver. 'Didn't see a thing', they say in chorus.

I'm hyperventilating. My wallet, my credit cards, address book. Why didn't I put my coat back on? How stupid can you get? A young policeman pokes his face out of the sliding door. 'Excuse me sir, my car ... My car has been stolen.'

Two parking men join us.

'What is the number of your car?' I don't know. I can't remember.

'What do you expect us to do, if you don't know the number?'

'I will go and ring my office.'

'Where exactly did you park it?'

'Right here ... only two minutes ago. Dear God, I left my coat too. I've lost everything.' The policeman shows little sympathy. He has seen it all before. 'People are stupid.'

I get angry. 'What sort of country is this? There is an organised gang at work here.'

I must get to a phone, ring my office, find out the number of my car. The phone booth has a view over the entrance which is one floor up. As I lift the receiver I see my car, neatly parked where I had left it. Dear God, how utterly stupid. I run towards the entrance. A parking attendant is just about to give me a ticket. I hop in and drive off. As I am leaving the airport a police car comes flying down the road. I'm immensely pleased I didn't give them my number.

Like so many things in life, this could have been a funny scene in a film. In fact when we try to recapture this, reality seeps away and a degree of distortion becomes almost inevitable.

China

I'm invited to be a jury member at the first International Film Festival in China. We have already visited the Forbidden City and the Great Wall, and are now flying to Shanghai. Across the aisle to my left is an ancient party official in uniform. He barks orders at everyone in sight. Two secretaries take notes. He must be an important man as the stewards kotow every time they walk past. The pilot pays him a visit and brings presents. The old man coughs and gasps, spits into a handkerchief.

We've landed in Shanghai and are ushered off the plane before the party official with his entourage. At the end of a long corridor of glass, a large contingency of press are waiting anxiously for the party member to make an appearance. We ask several people who this man is, but no one is willing to say. We try to stay as close to the glass wall as possible in order not to obscure the view for the press. The party member is very slow. He still hasn't appeared when we reach the end of the tunnel. We are to be met, so I look across to see if there's a chauffeur holding a sign with my name.

Suddenly I'm surrounded by the press and officials.

'Welcome to Shanghai. This is an historic moment. You're the first jury member to arrive for our first International Film Festival ... Please follow!' It still hasn't dawned on me that the reception is for us, until we are placed in front of a platform where an official gives a speech about the importance of this event. I've never been so embarrassed.

It's my turn to give a speech. 'Very pleased to be here.' Everyone applauds and cameras flash. Police cars with flashing lights whisk us off to our hotel.

We arrive at a large, peaceful estate in the middle of the city. 'This is where Mao used to stay and wrote part of his *Little Red Book*,' I'm told. Our suite has padded walls and a wide view over the surrounding parklands. Cranes gracefully stroll through the gardens. Gardeners clip the grass. Is this Mao's room? Am I sitting at his desk? This is holy ground.

The next day we have dinner with the jury members and officials. I'm sure our drinks have been laced. Spirits soar. Nagisa Oshima is presented with a 'golden penis award' and Oliver Stone asks the Mayor's wife if she ever slept with Mao. It's a mad evening that finishes up with us watching the old Shanghai jazz band playing tunes from the forties.

Sophia Loren arrives a few days later. Everyone knows she's famous, but no one knows what she looks like. Hector Babenco is asked if he's Sophia Loren and he says yes. He becomes alarmingly popular and distributes hundreds of Sophia's autographs.

We view a variety of films from all parts of the world. The South Korean film, *Sopyonje*, directed by Im Kwon-Tack, is the most stunning, moving masterpiece. How absurd that a film like this, with such depth and integrity, will never get a release in the western world.

The last night we drift along the river on a large boat. While the party is in full swing we hide in a corner with Oshima and talk about life and death and the cinema. Oshima is one of our most respected and important directors, yet he, too, finds it extremely difficult to find the funds for his next film. I remember how stunned I was watching *Empire of the Senses*, and here he is, sitting next to me, quietly sipping his whisky.

The hospitality of the Chinese and their great passion for the cinema shall not easily be forgotten. And when I get home, I must re-read Mao's *Red Book*. There must be a passage about the view from the window with the cranes and the trees and the many gardeners clipping the grass. I wouldn't mind staying here for a while to make an erotic film with Oshima about Mao's great passion for young maidens and his chaotic schemes to improve his world.

Friends, Foes and Some Chronological Order

When I first met Norman Kaye, he was doing a song and dance routine in a suburban theatre. My job was to photograph the performance and make some large blow-ups before opening night. I usually had twenty-four hours to produce the goods. Most of these plays were awful, but it was my first real contact with the theatre. It excited me and disappointed me at the same time. Norman was virtually in every performance, hamming it up. He was the star of the village theatre. One day he came to my little studio to order some prints. We talked, met again, never looked back. Somehow we grew up together — he was 45, I was 32. I admired his talent as a musician then more than his talent for acting. Norman acted! If only I could get him to relax.

I have always believed that if someone or something strikes the right chord in us, we can all soar. Norman gave me trust and love and understanding. He gave me confidence and gently steered me in the right direction. In return I offered him his own reality, and his performances in both *Lonely Hearts* and *Man of Flowers* are proof of this. Norman has appeared in most of my films. Even if there were no part for him, I would find some reason to have him around.

The actors and the director have to trust one another, especially when one makes films that try to explore the human condition in some depth. Ingmar Bergman and his friends are the best example of this. Together they achieve the purest fusion of talents ever to be expressed in the cinema.

The one thing I've learned after all these years is that I know nothing, that I mustn't know anything before I start filming. I sit in the locations, stare at the walls, imagine them come to life. Then the walls fold around the actors, embrace the action, become one. The time spent with the actors before every scene is crucial. I can't tolerate anyone else around and even distant noises can ruin my concentration. The actual form is then born in a few moments and all involved have contributed.

My first full feature, *Illuminations*, was produced by Tibor Markus, whom I'd met during *Don Quixote*. When not making movies, Tibor ran a wholesale business in cakes, but his heart and soul were in the movies. Tibor was passionate about everything he did, except his cake business. We had less than $20,000 to make a feature and needed all the help we could get. Tibor went around exchanging cakes for small or big favours. He inspired enormous enthusiasm in total outsiders with his charm and thick Hungarian accent. Once, while shooting miles away in the country, I mentioned that it would be nice to have a peacock standing by. Within an hour Tibor arrived with a peacock under his arm and a big grin on his face. The next day a large wild stallion appeared because the script required a horse. Tibor was one step ahead of everyone and everything, including himself.

We were looking for the male lead and as I had very little knowledge I left it up to Tibor to find the right man. One night he announced excitedly that I was going to meet a great talent called Tony Llewellyn-Jones. Tony arrived. We tried to explain the script to him. Nobody understood it, including me, but he said yes, he would do it. Many years later he admitted that, when Tibor rang him, he was convinced that Tibor was involved in pornographic movies; he only responded because of apprehensive but intrigued curiosity.

After completion of the film dear Tibor died in his sleep.

Tony became a wonderful collaborator, actor, producer, politician and friend. Together we established Illumination Films and throughout the last fifteen years we've worked together — sometimes separately for a year or two, but always returning to base. Without people like Tony and Norman, it would have been impossible to continue. Not to mention Bill Marshall, my lawyer and scrounger of finances, and Jim Khong who was, and always will be, more than a brother.

Our instincts seek human identity; and art, as they say, is a step towards the infinite. But to me the core of art is vision and kindness. Through vision we find divine origin in the sea, the sky, a single leaf, a drop of rain. And kindness brings us closer to the child, closer to the gods. These gods don't always need to be divine. The primitive, private passion of *Zorba the Greek*, for instance, is also part of the core of art. Romantic old fool dancing on the beach, knowing everything about life. It's all so simple. But what are we without him? It's so much better to run into Zorba's hairy arms, than to escape into the disco halls, wearing Pierre Cardin's underpants; to snuggle into Zorba's smelly armpits than to join the beautiful people splashing in the unpleasant, artificial blue of private swimming pools.

Yes, every film is a different journey. I've never been able to proceed unless the right station at the right time appeared along the tracks. *Kostas* dealt with the migrant and my growing

With Norman Kaye in India.

With Tony Llewellyn-Jones in Holland.

love for Greece; *Lonely Hearts* with the shyness of my adolescence; *Man of Flowers* with my childhood and growing obsession with beauty. Adelaide filmmaker Ian Davidson was the first person who supported the early filmmaking with cash, not words, and producer Phillip Adams was an important influence in getting *Lonely Hearts* off the ground, for which I shall always be grateful. The making of *Lonely Hearts*, however, proved a total nightmare and I decided to work with my own production company. So far, with the help of my friends, I've managed.

After *Lonely Hearts*, even with its success and worldwide release, it was difficult to get the next film going. I met an American producer who had worked out a new scheme to finance movies. Even obscure screenplays like *Man of Flowers* were considered. For six months, he kept me flying up to Sydney and back on a weekly basis. His scheme, which I never understood, would finance all pictures in the future. His scam collapsed, of course, and he disappeared before being arrested. We were left nursing *Man of Flowers* through the system and the system didn't want to know.

One day Jane Ballantyne, Tony Llewellyn-Jones and I decided to go solo. We hired an office, connected the phone and hung our company shingle, Flowers International, on the door. We lived the illusion of being in pre-production; ordered stock, looked for discounts, begged, borrowed and stole. Werner Herzog, a good friend ever since Michael Edols introduced us, came to stay for a while. He told me not to despair. 'Free the road ahead of all obstacles, whatever it takes', was his advice. Through Bill Marshall, our lawyer and co-conspirator, and with the help of dear friends, we managed to get together $240,000 in private money. A Russian emigré, Yuri Sokol, was director of photography. The painter Asher Bilu, an Israeli emigré, was art director. Both contributed enormously to the splendid look of the film. Norman Kaye was the man of flowers. The script was written for him. Chris Haywood played the painter who is immortalised in bronze. Since *Man of Flowers*, Chris has appeared in most of my films — one of the most versatile and ingenious actors around. Bob Ellis, with his sharp wit and brilliant sense of the absurd, helped me to complete the script and played a mad psychiatrist.

We were ignorant and fearless and went full blast into the night. Three weeks was all we had. Asher Bilu and his wife Luba generously offered us their house and everyone deferred and shared points. I don't think I slept at all during those three weeks. The film took its own course and all we could do was to follow the light and hope, hope that there would be an end to this madness. We were under enormous pressure.

I phoned Werner Herzog in Germany: 'One of us will have to play my father'. Werner was on the plane the next day and almost ripped the little boy's ear off in the first flashback. Werner took it very seriously and both he and the young boy are totally convincing. When Werner's brother Lucki saw the film later, he thought that Werner had portrayed his own father.

An old postcard with four well-dressed gentlemen watching the ocean and a sky full of seagulls had been pinned up on my wall for many years. It's one of those images that stay with you, have substance, keep feeding the imagination. I had no idea how to finish the film. The original ending didn't make sense any more. Too much had changed. One night during the shoot I walked up and down in my room and hit the naked lightbulb. The light kept dancing past this postcard on the wall. There was no sudden 'I've found it' elation. The image had simply found me. At the end of *Man of Flowers* this image becomes the painting, the mirror of life. Time has stopped and we gaze with the people into the distance and beyond.

In Ireland I met the English painter David Godbold. The same postcard features in one of his works. He'd also treasured this image

It's one of those images that stay with you, keep feeding the imagination.

for many years, carried it with him. He knew that one day it would inspire him by its serenity and strange beauty.

Jane and I went to Sydney to beg a recording company to allow us to use on the sound track their recording of Donizetti's *Lucia di Lammermoor*, with Jose Carreras and Montserrat Caballe. This music was crucial. Tony and I had spent endless nights listening to the many versions of *Lucia* that we had collected from all over the world. We knew that Maria Callas was out of our reach and Caballe moved us to tears;. I threatened to sit on the floor all night if they wouldn't make an immediate decision. The manager recognised that this was an emergency and gave us full rights.

I had never heard of the various categories in Cannes. We were invited to *un certain regard* which meant nothing to me. I flew there with Alyson Best, the female lead, and Jane arrived later It was my first time in Cannes and the first time I had seen the film with an audience on the big screen. By the end of the screening I was drenched in sweat, standing at the back, expecting everyone to hate it. Thunderous applause brought me out of my dark corner. For the rest of the week, the press chased me around town. It was the first time that I had to be 'public'. It was extremely unsettling. Soon afterwards I suffered a severe nervous breakdown.

Man of Flowers haunts me like the plague and is, strangely enough, still popular. It is a film that has its own light, its own darkness. Much of my early youth manifests itself through Charles, the protagonist. The critics were divided: some dismissed it as an oddball movie; others praised its lyrical beauty and undertook in-depth psychological investigations. A Belgian journalist, Jean-Pierre Wouters, hit the nail on the head when he called the film 'a painting of feelings'. I think he was right. Expressing feelings without using the language of words is the greatest challenge.

Meanwhile my marriage had collapsed. I was dreadfully disturbed. I wrote *My First Wife* while helping Werner Herzog with his film *Where the Green Ants Dream*, mainly at night, with a heart full of despair. Bob Ellis again came in to refine the screenplay. Contrary to common belief, *My First Wife* is not autobiographical. It deals with the terrible pain of separation — maybe with mine in particular — but the story does not in any way run parallel with the break-up of my marriage.

This time we had a reasonable budget, the luxury of a five-week shoot, Marianne Baillieu's studio at the waterfront as a perfect location, and the formidable talents of Wendy Hughes and John Hargreaves.

The sceds of *Cactus* have been discussed. When I met Isabelle Huppert in Cannes, I knew that the time had come to make the film. I had always admired Robert Menzies on stage and offered him the part of the blind man opposite Isabelle without a screen test. In fact I've never believed in screen tests. It's an humiliating experience for any actor and creates an enormous amount of mistrust. Robert had never acted in a film and the trust we shared reflects in his performance.

Whilst writing the script, Werner Herzog and I went to the airport to pick up Bruce Chatwin. Werner had expressed interest in one of his books and Bruce flew down to meet us. He talked like someone possessed. For twenty-four hours we sat around the dining-room table, mesmerised by his stories. I taped his theory on 'songlines' and used it later, with his permission, in the blind man's speech in *Cactus*.

Bruce popped up several times in the next few years. When *Cactus* had its premiere in Cannes, he phoned me from nearby and again talked for hours. He was already sick and dying, yet his enthusiasm was undaunted.

After his death I travelled through Holland and found his *Songlines* at a railway station. A man opposite me in the train said: 'That is a wonderful book; I've just read it.' At that very moment I read: 'The old woman's smile was like a message from the Golden Age. It had taught me out of hand to reject all arguments for the nastiness of human nature.' Bruce remained an optimist until his final breath.

I'm writing this book to exorcise a few demons, celebrate a few angels, explain my life more fully to my children; and in the hope of giving a few aspiring filmmakers some incentive to keep going. Some people one meets on the way, some books one reads, even some films one sees, are extremely important.

The little contact I had with Bruce Chatwin had a strong impact on me. He predicted that a film on Vincent van Gogh would be a 'tricky one'. Reason enough to tell the story ...

A few years before her death, my mother and I visited the Kröller-Müller museum in Holland, one of the most impressive museums in the world. You have to travel through a large forest to get there and when we finally arrived at the van Gogh collection, she was a little out of breath. She sat down in the middle of the room. There was nobody else around; we felt very privileged. I left her sitting there and started to view each painting carefully. When I'd completed the circuit, I arrived at Vincent's self-portrait. Of all his self-portraits, this one I find the most powerful. I stood there a long time. Then my mother quietly joined me. Vincent stared at us both with the most painful, hurt expression.

'There's such grief in his eyes ... such grief', she said softly. She started to shake, then a flood of tears — all-embracing tears. 'That great grief of humankind', as Vincent calls it in his letters, had totally overwhelmed her. It was there and then that I decided to make the film *Vincent, the Life and Death of Vincent van Gogh*.

When we got home, I discussed the idea with my sister Angeline and her husband Jaap and nothing more was said for quite a few years.

An American company expressed itself extremely interested and suggested that I talk to Michael Douglas, as his father had played Vincent some twenty-five years earlier. To use him would be a good sales gimmick, they said. This suggestion alone made it clear that we didn't have much chance of getting the money from the States. I saw this film as an homage to a great soul and didn't want either my ego or an actor's ego to interfere with Vincent's spirit. My approach was to have the whole film shot from his point of view: 'far too risky and experimental'. The US producers all agreed it was essential to have a big star play Vincent.

Then Linda Beath, a courageous Canadian woman who headed an American distribution company, helped us with the required pre-sale — or at least a promise of a reasonable pre-sale — and due to some favourable tax laws at the time, we managed to get the money together. In our offer document our pre-sale was mentioned, but we never had a signed contract. At this point I didn't give the legalities much thought — all would be sorted out by the time we'd finished the film.

I started to write the script like a man possessed. Too many years had gone by, too much fire and passion lost since the first conception. My co-worker and assistant, Millie Comfort, feverishly typed out the pages I produced in a room above her office. My daughter ran up and down with new pages and corrections. The initial burst delivered a finished script within two weeks and never required a second draft.

For the next two years, my friend and producer, Tony Llewellyn-Jones, and my steady companion, Brendan Lavelle, were virtually on the road in search of *Vincent*. Interiors and roster were done in Australia, but the tracing of Vincent's footprints had, of course, to be done in Europe. We had a deal with KLM airlines and flew back and forward to Europe.

It wasn't always easy to find the last century without a constant reminder of the times we live in. Even the most remote spot would have a plane in the sky or power lines spoiling the horizon. Every forest seemed full of empty beer cans and plastic bottles. We had a small van in which we travelled through the seasons. In the back, an old 35mm Arriflex movie camera with a solid tripod. Vincent's words travelled with us and gave us inspiration and guidance. I'd edited and sometimes retranslated his many letters and, in the process of doing this, automatically learned the script by heart. Each time a particular phrase or line matched the landscape we would bring the van to a screaming halt, set up camera and tripod — like easel and canvas — and record the landscape. I would at times whisper Vincent's words whilst filming in order to move the camera at the right speed.

One day a beautiful tableau of the last century appeared: an old shepherd leading his sheep through a yellow-green valley, half obscured in the early morning fog. The landscape behind him rolled on for miles without the obstruction of roads and power lines. Even the shepherd's clothing was from the last century. Someone remarked that if we had staged this for the film, it would have been an expensive scene, but it came to us as a gift, a gift from the gods. I was so moved that I fogged up the eyepiece and filmed without being able to see what was happening. The film opens with this shot.

With stunning precision Asher Bilu painted some remarkably original van Goghs; Bill Kelly meticulously drew the extra drawings needed for the film; and Oliver Streeton dedicated his gentle soul to the designs of the animation and graphics.

The editing of *Vincent* took approximately eight months. Apart from the filming, I also had to do the editing myself, as I was incapable of explaining how the film should be put together. After the first rough cut I flew to England to record John Hurt for the voice-over. For two days John exhausted his heart and soul and gave Vincent's words music. For Vincent's funeral half my family came to Australia. They, of course, had become very involved and — especially my sister Angeline and her husband Jaap — had given me tremendous support. Together with my father, my brother, Wim and Jaap's sister, Maria, they appear at Vincent's funeral, my father being the last person to follow the coffin out of the studio into the street.

The film critic Jay Scott came from Canada to play the dead Vincent. He looked so convincing that I later decided not to use an image of the dead body and removed it from the final cut. Unfortunately, I forgot to tell Jay about this and he was rather disappointed not to see himself appearing at the end. Then *Vincent* was completed and ready to travel.

We took him to Cannes and showed the first cut. It was a horrendous first screening: half the people walked out. The concentration span of the people in Cannes is notoriously poor, but we were dealing with a mass exodus! Afterwards, the few that had remained were silent and our American pre-sale was cancelled with the famous line: 'Beautiful film, Paul. But not for us … our company would never do it justice'. It was plain that the film had no sales potential and, according to one expert, wouldn't even get a video release. Who wanted to see a film on Vincent van Gogh without actually seeing the man?

Tony and I were left with a dead turkey and had to go home and face our investors. At first I was too stunned to realise what was happening. I thought we'd made an honest film that would move all those who knew a little about Vincent. Was I so totally mistaken? Even some of those close to us saw nothing worthwhile in the film and we found that very hurtful. Some investors threatened to sue. They soon saw that the promised pre-sale hadn't really existed and that the film's future looked grim. We borrowed more money to buy them out. I went into my usual post-film depression, only this time it was much more severe.

The end of a film is the end of a life. A deep melancholy paralyses my entire being. I often walk down to the sea from where my office is situated and find a similar melancholy lying over the sea. The sea, however, is free and limitless. In the midst of this, our endeavours seem so trivial. The enormous effort required to make a film suddenly has no meaning. 'Tragically meaningless amidst the immense aloofness of the universe.'

Locally the reception was also lukewarm. The film reviewer for the *Australian* at the time panned the film in a most insensitive and harmful way. After *Island* she repeated her attack. Many film festivals around the world, however, wanted to show the film. I decided to accept the invitations and travel with *Vincent*. Wouldn't let him out of my sight.

At the Vancouver Film Festival the film received a long standing ovation, which, after two years of intensive work and everything we'd gone through, moved me so deeply that I had to flee the cinema. I hid behind a truck parked across the road and watched the people leaving. That sudden appreciation had thrown me so badly that I couldn't remember the name of my hotel; I seemed to have lost my memory. I needed to find Hannah Fisher, the director of the festival. Suddenly someone was standing behind me. I recognised Anoja Weerasinghe, a wonderful Sri Lankan actress, in the dark. She'd understood my flight from the cinema and had simply followed me. One beautiful smile from her made the whole painful journey of *Vincent* and the initial disappointments disappear. Together we returned to the crowd and memory came back to me.

Tony and I had visions of courtrooms and jails and anxiously monitored *Vincent*'s critical success. Still no distributors were forthcoming. One reasonable offer had come in, but it evaporated. The problem was that this film had no violence, no sex, no humour, no drama, no fast action, no special effects, no stars — in fact, nothing at all that makes for a 'successful' film. But we stubbornly felt that we had something to give and not 'a product' to sell.

The Toronto Film Festival screened the film with great success. The audience loved *Vincent*. The critics were impressed but distributors were appalled. In the hotel lift, whist escaping an enthusiastic lady chasing me with a large sunflower I met Theo van Gogh, great grandson of Vincent's brother and a fine filmmaker in his own right. The absurdity of the situation made us friends for life.

In desperation I went to New York where the film was given a two-week season in a repertoire cinema. Andrew Sarris from the *Village Voice* devoted a full page to *Vincent* and called it: 'The most profound exploration of an artist's soul ever to be put on film'. God bless him. Our dead turkey had come to life. *Vincent* showed in cinemas across the States for well over a year. The film even starred on *Variety*'s Top Fifty list, which was rather comical. *The Hollywood Reporter* was also rather baffled. '*Vincent: The Life and Death of Vincent van Gogh* has been running continuously in the US for more than 42 weeks beating its nearest competitor by three months. Cox's film has admittedly only grossed just under $2 million but, then, *Vincent* is hardly your average commercial film. A stylized quasi doco-drama based on the readings from the artist's letters.' We never lost faith in our audience, in the individual and in *Vincent*. He never lost faith in us.

When *Vincent* could travel on his own, Kyra and I went to Greece. We needed to spend some time together, away from the world of film. It was a rich journey, full of light and tenderness. I realised again how important it was to listen to her, to find trust and peace together. We visited several islands, hired bicycles, swam

With Kyra on the boat to Astypalea, Greece.

in the blue ocean and then stayed for a long, endless summer month on Astypalea. Kyra was safe and well looked after by the local population. There were no roads to cross, no child molesters lurking in the dark, no drug pushers around the corner. She could freely explore the island without me having to worry.

I started to ponder the next film … couldn't help myself. I'd shot one of my early, little films here, one that had opened up so many roads and alleyways and convinced me I would become a filmmaker. The question: 'Where is home?' still hadn't been answered. This beehive on a hill was like a large womb of stone that made me feel protected and strangely at home.

I began to write a screenplay — again I called it *Island* — about a young woman coming to the island to kick a drug habit. Here she meets two other women from different parts of the world — a Sri Lankan devoted to her husband and her duties as a wife and mother, and a Greek devoted to her art and her independence. The screenplay was almost finished by the time we left and completed soon after our return.

A Canadian company decided to cover half the budget. This sort of confidence had never been placed in me before. I jumped at it. They liked the script. I wasn't so sure, but arrogantly thought there would be plenty of time to improve it once we got to the island. With deferments, some assistance from the Victorian Film Corporation and quite a few private investors, we were on our way. With Neil Angwin, art director and fellow dreamer; Paul Ammitzboll, grip, gaffer, handy-man and fellow producer; and Chris Haywood, actor and fellow madman; I went ahead to explore the location and set up the production. Chris was to play the part of Janis, a local deaf-mute who works on a building site. He needed to work with the deaf-mute on whom his character was based, and learn the local sign language.

In Athens we bought all we needed — so we thought — and

departed for Astypalea. Chris and I were standing on deck when the ancient village on the hill appeared. The sun was rising dangerously large behind the village, then suddenly emerged with endless streaks of gold. Chris had never visited these shores and was mesmerised. Alexandra, old friend and local production manager, had alerted the city fathers. We were welcomed by half the village and straight away taken to Michael's cafeneon for drinks and preliminary talks.

We had about three weeks before crew and cast were to arrive. Everything looked good. The local population showed great interest and were willing to participate. The setting itself was stunning. Chris Haywood worked with the deaf-mute and became so convincing that when his wife, Gillian, arrived and he helped her off the boat and carried her luggage, she didn't recognise him. Then the crew arrived, headed by Michael Edols as director of photography. Our regular DOP, Nino Martinetti, couldn't join us but Michael and I had a long-standing association which we both thought was strong enough to survive the challenges ahead. A few days later Irene Papas arrived. Thank God for Irene.

In Athens it was still sunny and warm. We had no idea that the weather could change so rapidly. Huge clouds were drifting in from the east, carrying thunder and rain. The rain was unseasonal and poured down ceaselessly. The ocean turned on us. Huge waves hit the shores and no other boat could enter the harbour. We became isolated from the rest of the world. The telephone system packed up one day and the fax refused to speak. The money we'd brought to the island was enough to see us through the first few weeks, but things got difficult when there was no sign of more forthcoming. I'd brought twenty crew members to the island, plus the actors.

After a week of shooting, I knew that we were facing a tough battle. Michael Edols, had his ideas and I had mine: it seemed we were working on two different films. Of course this created

Astypalea.

enormous tension. Fortunately, in time we reached a truce and later managed to repair the damage and become friends again.

A major cause of anxiety was that we never saw any rushes. The editor John Scott had nothing to assemble or edit. He supplied much needed comic relief by becoming the goat and dog wrangler. Once a tape arrived with pictures taken off the editing machine which more or less told us that the film was in focus. It was like being on a boat drifting in the ocean: whatever we tried to drag it back on course was doomed to failure.

On the very top of the island rests the Castro — the ruins of an ancient fort with two well-kept churches and a bell tower. To climb the tower on a windy day is extremely dangerous. Most of the people once lived in this confined space and many battles were fought with visiting Turks. 'Here the soil is drenched with our blood', I was told. No sensible soul would venture to the Castro at night. The wind howls and screams, can get so forceful that people have been literally blown off the ruins into the ocean below. Old doors and windows shriek and protest, create a symphony of terror. I tried to be brave one night and visited the Castro on my own. Within ten minutes I was back in the safety of the village square. I'd seen the devil. Jim Currie, our sound man, was the next victim. He returned completely ashen — couldn't manage to record any sound and was attacked by a wild force that tore out his heart. The villagers were right. This was holy ground, committed to both God and the devil.

The pressure and lack of organisation became too much. The only person who stood his ground and kept us going was Paul Ammitzboll. The picture would never have been completed without him. By the third week of the shoot, we were becoming hysterical. One day Norman Kaye inadvertently changed one of his lines. His character's dog had died three months earlier, but Norman made it three hours. I became helpless with laughter, couldn't stop for a full day. A large amount of film was wasted on an essential scene and had to be discarded in post-production.

The incident recalled another during the filming of *Lonely Hearts* which had brought on a similar attack, also in the third week of shooting. Inner tension builds up and when something goes wrong or takes an unexpected turn, I can lose all reason. Julia Blake, with her marvellous, instinctive sense of humour, wrinkled her nose in distaste at the 'smell' of her brother Peter's (again Norman Kaye's) dog. It was enough to put me out of action for hours.

Meanwhile my fingers had started to bleed badly. The wounds would close at night and were still fine in the morning, but as soon as I got out of bed they would open up and wherever I went trails of blood would follow. Three doctors on the island couldn't help me. They had never seen anything like it

It started to become clear that I'd pushed my luck a little too far. When we finally returned to Athens news came that the exposed film and equipment had been lost. The bleeding started again. After an anxious three days we learned that most of the film had arrived in Australia. A few crucial cans have never been found.

I watched *Island* again, recently. There are some terrible holes in the film, but a few very fine scenes will live. Irene Papas subduing the deaf-mute, Chris Haywood, for instance; Eva Sitta talking to the old couple; and Anoja Weerasinghe's scream in the village square after she hears that her husband has been murdered.

A Woman's Tale, The Nun and the Bandit, Exile, Lust and Revenge

For the painter it can be hard to find the money to pay for canvas and paint, for the sculptor to buy the tools to carve into the rock, for the dancer and the musician to find a stage and an audience. The writer is probably the most fortunate in terms of costs, but here the inner struggle can be the demon.

The filmmaker might have a lot in common with the other artists, but nothing is more brutal and immediate than the need for money, lots of money. The filmmaker needs support, investments, is dependent on funding bodies and government hand-outs. And with the need for money, comes all the greed, hatred and ignorance the world has to offer. The art of making films doesn't really exist. It's 'this business of making films' that counts. The big question is: 'Is it commercial?' Then: 'What audience do you have in mind? How are you going to market it?' The responsibility to make a film commercially viable drains all vision, all illusion. We have to bribe, beg, pray and hope. Fight a bureaucratic war that has no end, and patiently listen to those in charge of the money: officials, exhibitors and distributors who decide what and whose film should be made and what is 'commercial'.

Most of these people do their best and can't help the system; others viciously oppose independence, are appallingly ignorant. I once returned from Greece with the happy tiding that Mikis Theodorakis had granted me the rights to one of his songs for free. My friend Takis Emmanuel had made this possible. 'Who is Mikis Theodorakis?' I was asked by the film executive in charge.

The federal funding body had conceived the plan of each year fully financing a group of selected films without their having to first secure the usual pre-sales and up front deals. Twenty million was put aside to make five films at approximately four million each. In my view it should have been twenty films at one million. In the first year we applied with a film project called *Homecoming*, starring Irene Papas. I went for an interview and was informed that our chances were high — stand by for action!

The next day, a phone call. We'd just missed the boat. The panel had decided to go for the youth market. I couldn't argue with that. The next day another phone call. One film had fallen through and we were again in the running. Could I please get Irene Papas to send a resumé and a letter of intent? I was embarrassed to ask such an eminent actress as Irene; but nevertheless I telephoned her in the middle of the night and she generously complied. Two days later I was informed that they'd sorted out the mess and once again we were not in the lottery.

Each one of the five films made that year lost more than the four films I made much later with this funding body's help, yet finally I was told not to come back, as my films had returned too little to be taken seriously. 'We're not a cultural institution; we're a film bank.'

Making films about the human condition that are idiosyncratic and personal is a tricky business. 'Experts' assess the scripts and usually advise other 'experts' not to go ahead. I never made a film that didn't go through several condemnations. I used to keep a file of rejections. *Lonely Hearts* was rejected by every funding body I approached. Assessments of the script were terrible; it had no commercial appeal. Finally, Phillip Adams, after he saw *Kostas*, was courageous and mad enough to back it. The film was named Best Film of the Year by the Australian Film Institute and had much commercial success.

The safest thing to do is to shut up, obey the rules and obey those in charge, modify ideas and ideals and hide dreams and illusions. Critical success — especially abroad — is fatal. It makes people envious, suspicious and when financial success doesn't immediately follow critical success, no 'next film' will be forthcoming.

Once I received a letter from our local funding body:

> It is known that you have global audiences and we appreciate having a filmmaker of your stature living here but we had hoped that your international reputation could deliver more international finance into your pictures ...

There are, of course, some marvellous souls, like Judith McCann, Head of the South Australian Film Corporation, who fight all the odds and have taste and compassion, vision and generosity of spirit. Judith managed to secure the tail end of the financing of *Shine* and put herself on the line to see the film made.

No civilised country expects their ballet company or opera company to make a profit — or at least used not to. These days things have changed. I wonder what would have happened to true filmmakers like Luis Bunuel, Ingmar Bergman, Michelangelo Antonioni, Federico Fellini etc., if they had been obliged to start their career in the present climate. They would have had too many problems now getting their films made; most likely they would have stopped fighting the odds and done something more sensible.

Once at an American university I mentioned the films of Bunuel. Out of a class of thirty only three had heard of him. No one had seen any of his films. It's a bit like teaching English and finding that your students have never heard of Shakespeare — or teaching music without knowing about Mozart. This may have been an exception but this type of ignorance is widespread amongst the decision-makers of Hollywood. I've met many film executives, vice-presidents, senior vice-presidents, CEOs etc who have no idea about the cinema in general and the possibilities of the medium in particular.

Quite a few times I've been offered support from abroad. Fully financed deals with generous above-the-line figures. But they always involved 'embracing the larger picture', dropping local support, being disloyal to my friends, the actors and crew; and 'reaching for the stars'. In the light of this, it's rather frustrating to find myself regarded by the local government authorities as difficult, too arty and too much of a financial risk.

Once an idea or a particular image has presented itself, it seems to have a will of its own. No matter how you try to pull out the roots, it creeps back like ivy, latching on to the subconscious with terrible determination. 'The painting' has been conceived, screams out to be born; but there's no canvas, no paint. Any other artist has the chance to start with 'the painting'; the filmmaker must keep the fire burning while looking for paint, brush and canvas.

My son Ezra wrote once:

> I'm not a believer of fate. I believe in contingency, a world of accidents like dust motes floating in air. Some of which are inhaled, others glide away, never seen. That's why one's life should always play out a story, so that the dust motes we collide with can be deciphered and always remind a person that he in fact lives, though to what end remains a mystery.

To solve that mystery I have to make a film. *A Woman's Tale* is one of those mysterious journeys that had to be made. We must live life with all our senses, otherwise we deny all depth and beauty of existence. This was Sheila Florance's motto. She lived and breathed by it. I'd seen her once on stage: her formidable presence always lingered. We were friends for many years. She played small parts and always complained about them.

'When am I starring in one of your films?'

One day I met a mutual friend, Dawn Klingberg, in the street. Dawn told me that Sheila was very sick, dying from cancer. I was on the way to meet Maria, my friend and cleaning lady. As I climbed the stairs, I came across the flat of an old woman living below Maria. The door was wide open. A fire had raged through the place. The woman was looking through her charred belongings, putting blackened objects that were dear to her in a plastic bag. She had long white hair, eyes full of tears.

In the hallway were two social workers. One whispered: 'We'll give her another ten minutes'.

Maria told me that the woman had fallen asleep whilst cooking dinner. The whole building almost had gone up in flames. She was now a risk and had to be removed to an old people's home. The image of this old woman standing in the midst of her burned-out home, surrounded by unrecognisable objects that were dear to her, struck me like a spark from her fire.

That night I went to see Sheila. We didn't talk about her illness, laughed a lot, drank lots of wine. Before I parted, she reminded me that there was still time to 'make her a star'. As soon as I got home, I started to write the screenplay for *A Woman's Tale*. The first draft took three days and three nights. Then Barry Dickins joined me, with his fine wit and humanity. Sheila added many personal touches. The whole process might have taken four weeks.

How were we going to get this financed? How could we persuade anyone to give us just $800,000 to make a film about an old woman who dies in the end? No commercial potential and the actual star was literally dying! After some deliberation, a small percentage was secured with deferments and a little private support. With the help of Bill Marshall and co-workers Sonny Naidu and Paul Ammitzboll, we managed to persuade the federal funding body to help us. I must emphasise that if we'd tried to get the money at a later point in my career, it would not have been possible. Then, my reputation still had potential dollars signs attached to it, and helped for a change. A first-time filmmaker would have been laughed at.

We had two thirds of the budget. I underwrote the distributor and lied about Sheila's state of health to get a completion guarantee. I lied about the script, I lied about the budget, I lied about everything. When Sheila was told she had approximately eight weeks to live we decided to go ahead. One week was lost because the guarantee wasn't in place. Lots of things weren't in place, but we had to proceed.

Before we started, Paul Grabowsky wrote a beautiful film score. This was the first time I'd actually used a composer. I asked Sheila not to die on me. 'If you die, you will kill me.' She promised to be a good girl. We filmed for four weeks in my own apartment. Sheila was in every frame. She was everywhere, larger than life. It became very much her film, a wonderful celebration of her life. The crew was immensely supportive, strangely emotional. Nino Martinetti, our DOP, created the most poignantly memorable images and Gosia Dobrowolska, as Sheila's confidante and co-conspirator, turned in a performance of magic and radiance.

Before, during and after the making, I was told once again: 'This will never sell'. Someone even claimed we were making a 'snuff movie'. The film was completed in time and fell together seamlessly. For an art-house film *A Woman's Tale* was enormously successful. It sold to many countries and was received with great praise by critics

Sheila Florance.

around the world. It won the Australian Human Rights Award and the Grand Prix at the international film festival in Ghent. The only bad review came from one local film critic who condemned the film on all fronts. This was once again a film that had none of the ingredients that make a successful movie, nothing to tantalise the senses.

The film gave Sheila a new lust for life. She lived for another six months, long enough to collect her well deserved AFI Best Actress Award. Her wit and stamina were pungently expressed in her brief acceptance speech: Betty Hutton's famous phrase: 'It's too much, too soon.' More than any of the other films I wanted *A Woman's Tale* to succeed, to be seen and shared. This was Sheila's film. Her tribute to the indomitable spirit and the beauty of life.

Right through *A Woman's Tale* there are flashbacks, or rather, dream-images of Sheila walking through a forest — a white forest. Sometimes she's alone, sometimes a young hand appears. At the edge, through the woods, there are some children running past — calling, playing, teasing. Sometimes the forest appears from Sheila's point of view. These images have nothing to do with the story, are shot in a totally different way, are slotted in almost at random and at the end are shared by her friend and soul mate Anna, the nurse — Gosia Dobrowolska. Nobody ever asked me what these images meant; they are accepted, because they come from within Sheila's character.

Rainer Maria Rilke said: 'Young forests don't exist.' Sheila said: 'White forests don't exist, except in my dreams.' All through her life she had had a re-occurring dream of being caught in a small, white forest. I'd spotted the forest we used some years earlier on a friend's property. Almost white, bleached out trees, twisted and gnarled like rope. I had always known I would return one day.

I visited Sheila in hospital a few days before she died. We both knew this was the last time.

'What a lovely day outside. Why don't we flee through the back door and escape in your car?' she said.

'Yes, let's, but where to?'

'That's the problem, isn't it?' She was so frail. Her eyes had grown very large in her withered face.

'There is still so much love in me. It's oozing from me, filling this room', she whispered. 'What are you going to do with it? No, no tears, please — I love you.'

'I love you too, very much.'

I went outside into that beautiful day, walked home through the parks, the busy streets. The next day, I went back to the hospital to pick up my car. Three parking tickets were decorating the windscreen. I left them flapping in the wind as I drove home.

A year after its completion, *A Woman's Tale* had its first United States screening in New York as part of a major retrospective of my films at the Lincoln Center. Across the street from my hotel I could look into the many apartments of an old building and follow the routines of the inhabitants. People moved in and out of shadows, opened and closed doors, drew their blinds when night came. In one apartment the lights were always on, the blinds always open. A young, naked woman would lie on her stomach watching television. It didn't matter what time I got up or came home, she was there in the same position. Observing her increased my sense of isolation and loneliness. There were quite a few official engagements and Wendy Keys, the director of the Center, was warm and kind and supportive, but I felt alone and disturbed. I missed sharing this event with Sheila, with all those people who had helped me throughout the years. Almost every film I'd ever made was being shown. This was my life, or what had happened in my life. I wanted my mother to be there.

One night the naked girl across the street curled up in a foetal position and started to cry. I could see her whole body shaking. Why was she always naked? Why was she alone? Why was she crying? She came to the window and pressed herself against the glass. Her body was very small now, child-like, distorted. I could feel her immense pain going out into the night. A loud siren from a passing ambulance drew her away from the window. Then she closed the blinds. They remained closed until my departure.

The *New York Times* wrote:

> There's no sense of embarrassment or disgust when we view Martha in her bathtub, her hands touching her shrunken, dwindling flesh in amaze, as though she can't quite believe it is the shape she now inhabits. Later, when Martha and Anna, both nurse and friend, swim together in a pool, Cox catches some primal continuity in ripe maiden and desiccated crone afloat in the same life-sustaining medium. So vivid is Florance's character, it seems the cruelest kind of cheat that this rare being, full of wisdom and appetite it's taken a lifetime to achieve, should be switched off by death.

In 1997 — six years later — I'm promoting *A Woman's Tale* in Japan. Sheila is alive and well-loved and respected. Here's that little film we made in the face of death deeply touching the Japanese. Etsuko Takano, the courageous woman who brought the film to Japan, expects it to have a long run. The press reacts strongly, the story is so relevant here. I feel as passionate about *A Woman's Tale* as when we first completed it, and I feel Sheila's presence. We're promoting it together.

The Japanese think deeply about life, though rarely verbalise their thoughts. Sheila makes them speak and open up. Someone told me that he'd achieved a certain respectability in life, but had suffered deeply. He claimed that another person would never be able to perceive the degree which he'd suffered, because 'He's another person and not me'. For many years he'd harboured this very thought, but then he'd seen Sheila's courage and lust for life and the uniqueness of his suffering had suddenly left him. 'I feel relieved and less alone', he said.

In his book *Voltaire's Bastards*, John Ralston Saul argues that Western civilisation is without belief, for the first time since the decline of the Roman Empire. 'We've killed God and replaced him with ourselves.'

I found this book while visiting the Toronto Film Festival and became so engrossed that I missed seeing some dear friends. Maybe if I'd read the book elsewhere, it wouldn't have had such an impact. Toronto is very dear to my heart and the Festival has played an important part in introducing my films to a wider public.

'Civilisation cannot survive without belief; without spirit and faith we're doomed.' It made me contemplate a religious move, a shift towards a more devotional or ceremonial cinema. The worst move of my career. I don't regret it.

On Hydra in Greece lives a man called Don Lowe — a man who for some thirty years has sat on a rock and written compulsively about the earth, the sky and his loneliness. One could fill a small bookshop with his collective works, yet nothing he has written has ever been published. Don doesn't mind; he's the one that stated:

'I keep feeding the vultures, even though they're feasting on my bones.'

Don is a writer. That's his belief, his religion. His God is the God of creation. Don is also mad, a fine, compassionate madness all too rare in a Godless world. One day, on one of his excursions to the mainland, Don walked into a second-hand bookshop in Athens and, intrigued by the title *The Nun and The Bandit*, purchased an old copy for twenty drachmas. For the next fifteen years he contemplated its content and finally wrote a screenplay based on this novel by E.L. Grant Watson.

Don's screenplay did not inspire me. I tried to push it onto others without success. But when an old copy of the novel arrived with the blessing of Grant Watson's daughter, Josephine Spence, I found myself drawn into the intoxicating landscape of a true visionary. Here was the material I was looking for. 'Civilisation cannot survive without belief; without spirit and faith we're doomed.' Grant Watson's belief and religion originated in the personification of the powers of nature. His cathedral was the landscape — large, vast and all-embracing. His God was the God of spirit and faith, nourished by his senses. The Father, the Child and the Ghost permeated his being, his spirit and the landscape.

I reduced the book to a minimal screenplay and made an almost minimalist film, based on an old-fashioned, religious topic, directing my prayers towards the powers working behind the phenomena of nature, instead of towards the God of my youth. 'Believing in the one God, makes one blind towards the other gods.' Maybe this is what happened in the process of making *The Nun and the Bandit*. The film was badly received, but this did not deter me from adapting another of Grant Watson's novels, *Priest Island*. To honour Don's lonely cry from the rocks, I followed his advice and called it *Exile*.

Although the ground was a little shaky after *The Nun and the Bandit*, I managed to whip up enough support for *Exile* and in no time we were on our way to Tasmania, another island that would prove difficult to conquer.

Every time I make a film, I start enthusiastically to write a diary. Try to keep a record of what goes on around me and inside. Every time I only get a few pages down. As soon as the film takes over, a silence falls and the notes stop. These notes on *Exile* might throw a little light on the state of mind I was in.

1 March 1993: Another ten days to go before we set out on our next adventure, *Exile*. After *The Nun and the Bandit* this film has been lingering and has somehow found its way to the surface. I went back to the island of Astypalea, to write the screenplay. The view from the room of the house I stayed in was important as it contained all the elements relevant to the story. A large sky with a continuous movement of clouds. From small, white puffs to large, dark cloudships carrying thunder and rain. Then there was a small edge of the ocean, only visible when I raised my head. The rest was taken up by a square building with a tiny room on top. Now and then an old man would appear. He would stand there for a long time checking the ocean and the sky and the surrounding hills. He was a retired sea captain with a head full of nostalgia.

We have a splendid cast and much enthusiasm from all involved. There are still many logistics to be dealt with but slowly we are getting things sorted out. When I think of the enormous task ahead of me, I feel a cold, clammy hand on my heart. But we must stand tall and proceed. Even at this stage of my life I can so easily plunge back into that void, that helpless black hole that appears when we can't find any answers to the big questions of life and the horrific crimes of mankind.

5 March 1993 One more weekend to sort things out. I cannot look at the script any longer. Cannot concentrate on anything at all. Slowly everything is going blank, an emptiness that will protect me. 'And in the one arose love. Love, the first seed of soul.'

Who knows the truth? Were the gods here before the universe? Darkness is hidden in darkness. The 'it' is breathing within, breathing by its own power. We will travel through the flesh to holiness.

The trucks have been loaded and have just departed. I'm forced to talk to people to keep the organisation going. Everything is cold and distant. I'm existing in a cruel void and wait for help — not from outside but from within.

11 March 1993: We managed to get on the boat and during the night crossed Bass Strait. Not many of us slept. I'm sure it's not because of the upcoming adventure. The tiny room here has no portholes; it doesn't feel like being on a boat. You can feel that this used to be a big, proud boat with much space and atmosphere. With the refurbishing they stripped the boat of all strength and beauty. I'm sure that's the reason we didn't sleep. A boat journey could be or should be colourful, like the many journeys I have made on the liners to the Greek islands.

12 March 1993: We drove across Tasmania to get to our base. This is the third time I've come here and it feels good and right. This is the spot where we shall find our *Exile* and find our god. The mountains in front of my window are growing larger as the light travels across the sky. The water down below is still, no wind, no noise. The occasional cry of a strange looking bird is the only contact with reality.

Now I'm sitting in an A-shaped house with a second bedroom as an office, and a view that stuns the senses and the heart. An evening glow has spread its flames over the wide expanse of the bay in front of me. Worked out the first important shot and although understood by most, found others who couldn't see, reluctant to flow with the 'moulding of the wound'. A scar is being engraved on the rocks — a 'collective scar' that must not have the imprint of myself or any other individual.

No more motivation, no more questions, no more answers. We must trust our instincts. We managed to work out what the ghost should wear and what he represents. Norman Kaye is totally with me. It's so good to have an instinctive togetherness. I need his understanding, his love and his compassion. My companion and soul mate is not acting now, but doing wardrobe, which has been difficult for her. But she's done a splendid, committed job and is now in charge of her operations. As an actress it must be very hard to be on the other side of the camera. I can feel her void.

15 March 1993: For three days now I have tried to find the time to write. That has not been possible. Whatever goes through one's head before a film is pretty horrendous.

Today was the first day of shooting. It's not possible, ever, to know what we have caught. I feel confident, though, and have faith. I'm extremely tired and suffer a severe pain in both my knees.

17 March 1993: Early morning, waiting for the first laboratory report. I have the feeling that something special is happening, good or bad — who knows. I believe special. The sea is extremely calm. The sky remains overcast, like a Dutch sky in winter. Large skies with now and then a pale sun managing to break through. An overcast sky is much more mysterious than an open sky, much more far reaching.

20 March 1993: It's impossible to find the time or the energy to write. This is a very demanding time and maybe my body is getting too old to climb up and down the mountains and stand upon the rocks. But much is in the mind and when one feels strong enough mentally, the highest mountain can be conquered.

Jim Currie, our sound man and, since *Man of Flowers*, also the sound designer and mixer of my films, is obsessively recording separate waves. 'There's a whole symphony out there', he tells me. Jim's enthusiasm and love is of great comfort. He's an essential link, sharing the same faith.

Now the wind howls endlessly. I looked at the sea today through the camera — just a small patch of ocean — and I felt overwhelmed. The pattern of the seaweed being tossed around by the water. Every move, every movement, every pattern was perfect. It all related to the nervous system inside the body, in the brain, in the heart. Why can't we see? Sometimes I'm scared to continue and just want to hide and return to my children.

'All that you're seeking is also seeking you.'

That's all there is. A few more clumsy scribbles that I can't decipher. The film has to tell the rest.

Exile was made with a young cast: Aden Young, Claudia Karvan, Beth Champion, David Field. Norman Kaye played the ghost and Chris Haywood a priest of obsessive righteousness. With Aden I had a memorable fight, high on the rocks that sealed our friendship.

My relapse into religion, or rather investigation into new holy ground, caused three bitter years of rejections and lack of faith within me and all around me. I had to sell my house, worked as a labourer and handy man and reshaped my old flat above the office.

Together with Janette Turner Hospital, I developed a screenplay called, *Suicide of a Gentleman*. We had most things in place, and already much pre-production money and energy had been spent. I'd counted on support from our local film body but, without warning, this was denied. It was the first time Janette had become involved in the film world and I regret the fact that my collaboration with such a fine writer never came to fruition.

Judith McCann saved me from total despair by encouraging *Lust and Revenge*. I went full circle when my old comrade and co-writer of *Lonely Hearts*, John Clarke, joined me to write the screenplay. John helped me to restore my faith, to replace God with ourselves and laugh again.

Lust and Revenge is a satire about art, money and sex. We could have taken it a bit further, but my desire for revenge had almost evaporated by the time we refined the screenplay. To carry a grudge for too long hurts the heart. Hatred only harms the person who

Exile *with Aden Young.*

hates. Some major characters that I'd wanted to expose had become too insignificant. John and I decided to embrace a larger picture. We went for the art scene in general and the manipulation of the artist in particular.

Many friends from the past supported me. Wendy Hughes dressed up as a man and became an arts adviser to tycoon Chris Haywood. John Hargreaves, dying with AIDS, joined the production as the gallery 'sleaze'. A witty and courageous performance — it was to be his last. Pamela Rabe set the satirical mood in a small part at the beginning and Hugo Weaving played another insane psychiatrist. Unfortunately we had to eliminate him from the final cut, as we had one psychiatrist too many. Gosia Dobrowolska went completely against type and portrayed Cecilia, a religious fanatic, with great zeal and conviction.

Apart from Nicholas Hope, Bryan Dawe and Ulli Birve, I'd worked with all the other actors for many, many years and even John Larkin — co-writer on other scripts — became an actor of dubious merit. It was a great demonstration of solidarity and did much to help me regain my confidence. Actors are considerably more loyal than the average film person.

I underwrote the distribution guarantee myself. Paris-based Jeannine Seawell, who's done so much ground-breaking work to put the Australian film industry on the world map, was not accepted as underwriter by the Film Finance Corporation unless she guaranteed some $200,000 for distribution so I made a deal with Jeannine and guaranteed her the money. An enthusiastic and supportive Belgian distributor, Alexander Vandeputte, pre-bought the film rights for the Benelux countries and then the FFC finally accepted our proposal. Before proceeding, however, they demanded proof of my track record. I made photocopies of hundreds of clippings and reviews in many languages and couriered these to them. Such a large record of achievement was not enough security:

At the last minute they also demanded seventy per cent of the territory of Germany. I was in for a rough ride but didn't see any alternative. Had it been known that I'd underwritten the distribution guarantee myself, the whole production would probably have been canned. Maybe I should have been caught because now, two years later, I'm still paying off the debt incurred.

I'd teamed up again with Jane Ballantyne and had a devoted Adelaide crew. The trouble was, though, that I couldn't relate to the various characters who manipulated or were being manipulated. They were too close to the real thing.

The South Australian distributor, Barry Loane, put himself on the line to make the film work and Australia took kindly to *Lust and Revenge* — welcomed it with critical acclaim and a reasonable box office. David Stratton, who for so many years has encouraged and supported me, was the first to praise the film in *Variety*. One would think that I was back on track, but the federal financing body didn't think so and advised me not to present my next film project, *Innocence*, to them.

Australia doesn't really have its own film industry because we shy away from our identity and the people who could reflect this identity. Our best-known filmmakers, like Peter Weir, Fred Schepisi and Bruce Beresford, had to go abroad. If they hadn't, they would have suffered total alienation and their experience and technical brilliance would sadly have been wasted.

People with a recognised body of work are treated with a great degree of suspicion. Producers can produce one turkey after another, but once a director fails, he or she is in big trouble. But these are the people who, in the end, actually make the movie. Usually these people have very vulnerable hearts, and battle their insecurity as much as anyone else — usually more so. Is it any wonder that these insecurities manifest themselves sometimes in arrogance and a ridiculous sense of superiority? I've been accused of biting the hand that feeds me. There's some truth in this. Maybe it was a bit much to expect continuous support.

When it became known that I'd accepted to make a film in 3-D for the IMAX Corporation, I received several stunned reactions. One came from a struggling filmmaker in Germany. 'I'm deeply disappointed. You're one of the few who kept me wanting to continue ... who remained independent and didn't sell out. Why do something so blatantly commercial now?'

There's nothing 'blatantly commercial' about *The Hidden Dimension*. Ulli Beier wrote a book, *Ten Thousand Years in a Lifetime*, about Albert Maori-kiki, a New Guinean who'd travelled from the Stone Age to the New Guinea parliament in half a century. Why then, couldn't I travel from my rubber-band factory to the very latest in film technology? It also coincided with a desire to work outside of Australia, to get away from a bureaucracy that was making it more and more difficult to keep being a filmmaker.

The Hidden Dimension wasn't a call from Hollywood. The producers were dedicated, talented people who were idealistic about their movie and gave me much trust.

It has been said that all activity of man begins as dream and then becomes dream once more. The painter Giorgio de Chirico said that his life, and thus his dreams, were always three-dimensional, and claimed to paint in 3-D. When I accepted the IMAX challenge, I remembered de Chirico's bold statement. I stood for many hours in front of his paintings, sometimes with wide-open eyes, sometimes with half closed eyes, sometimes closed eyes. I saw no 3-D forthcoming. But de Chirico led me back to Vermeer. With chalk lines Vermeer achieved what I now see as 'perfect perspective'. The very key to the magic of 3-D.

We were trying to film an ordinary story with ordinary people. The IMAX three-dimensional format would make it extraordinary. The film is about a quest undertaken by a young girl — as set by her grandfather — to encourage her to see more deeply into life. The 'hidden dimension' refers to the millions of microscopic life forms which share our lives as another universe. It was very important to make the people feel and look real. Any 3-D distortion would cheapen the film.

The idea of perfect perspective at first seemed impossible. The camera had to 'dance' as well, and how do you make a camera dance when you need four people to carry the bloody thing? In addition to its clumsiness, this camera is a real beast which still hasn't been tamed. It growls so loudly that in small spaces the actors can't even hear one another speak. Endless patience, endless rehearsals, endless technical challenges. Our three protagonists, Charlotte Sullivan, Gosia Dobrowolska and C. David Johnson, persevered, remained cool, and stood their ground.

The IMAX format gives us images that are immensely beautiful. We are guided into an extraordinary world where the eye can travel, explore, find poetry. It has all the signs of being the great new medium for the twenty-first century. It is a glorious medium which draws us right inside the picture. There is nothing virtual about this reality.

Our approach caused a few frowns amongst the IMAX hierarchy. Barbara Kerr, John Larkin, Margot Wiburd and myself repeatedly rewrote the script. I'd never worked in an atmosphere of such insecurity. The man in charge wanted the script to be 'snappy'. 3-D is not a snappy medium. I tried to shoot our film in such a way that little could be done to destroy its heart.

I was warned that to work with a large crew and many technicians would be difficult, but I found the whole process most rewarding. The production team and I were on the same wavelength; all we had to do was stay away from the experts in Armani suits. The film was almost unanimously well received, with great critical acclaim. IMAX produced a special brochure citing all the marvellous reviews. This was apparently too much for our executive officer, who wrote an amazing article in the IMAX magazine to justify his belief that the film 'wasn't what the audience wanted.'

It started by saying, 'People are human and therefore make mistakes ...' The title was wrong. It was he who chose the title 'Four Million House Guests', not me. *The Hidden Dimension* was my choice. Further, the pace was too slow, according to various surveys. Yet he'd also discovered that audience satisfaction was very high. He was committed to releasing films that 'have broad appeal, satisfy a theatre's mandate and deliver at the box office ...' Yet 'A film that stimulates the audience's senses and challenges each person to view his or her surroundings with open eyes and an open mind has enormous value.' How can one compete with an ego of such contradictions? An audience — especially an audience of children — needs to be respected. They need to be allowed to interpret the story themselves, find their own dreams.

The Children

You may well wonder why hardly any of the women who were important to me and were a strong motivating force in my life, featured or were mentioned. I don't think it fair to dig into the past of relationships and talk about the intimacies that belong to two people. I also feel that I have no right, no reason to implicate others. This is not a 'kiss and tell'. My reasons for writing these reflections lie elsewhere.

From the early beginnings as a photographer and later as a filmmaker, I often confused my passions and obsessions. Drifted in and out of my creations without realising the personal demands upon the people close by, or their expectations. It took many years and much pain outside and within to achieve some balance. Everything was meant to be — the merging and the separations. Let there be no bitterness between us. Life clears like the sky. After much deliberation, though, I feel I need to reflect on the mothers of my children and how these children came into the world.

Ezra

Before my friend Elwyn went to Indonesia in the early seventies, I urged him to visit the Borobodur in Java; a mysterious temple for many years hidden in the jungle and rediscovered by some Dutch explorers. An eerie feeling of *déjà-vu* had puzzled me on an earlier visit and left a lasting scar.

In the bus on the way there, Elwyn sat next to Elisabeth. They talked, connected and explored the sights of the temple together. Elisabeth promised to come and see him during a short stopover in Australia on her way to the States. Meanwhile, I'd photographed some of Elwyn's sculpture and had the finished prints waiting for him on his return. He told me about this woman he had met on the bus; he wanted me to meet her. He'd thought of me intensely, he said, as he explored the Borobodur with her. A few days later Elisabeth arrived. Elwyn invited her to my studio.

It is a long time ago now since she walked through the door — many centuries — but I remember very clearly that sudden singing of my blood. We talked for six days and six nights. The seventh day we loved. She'd been scheduled to stay for two days but her airline had gone on strike. Then she left with a vague promise to return. I was heartbroken. Imagined her arms always around my head. I had given her a little box I'd found as a child in the ruins of our town. A brass box with a dented lid. She handed me a small brass animal with one ear missing. She called it 'the beast'. I decided always to carry it with me.

Two letters arrived. 'Don't put your thoughts of me away', she wrote. Then nothing for many months. I longed and wondered ... wandered the world without being able to put my thoughts of her away. Two years later she made contact again and invited me to Berlin. I went. It was awful to see her. Everything had grown so distant, so cold. We couldn't look at one another. Clumsy words, shy smiles, an empty house. Her two cats sat on a cupboard eyeing me with mistrust. On the table we had put our little gifts. The brass box and that little animal with a missing ear.

As we parted, I tried to kiss her lips but she turned away and my kiss landed on her cheek. Then I found myself in the cold, icy streets of Berlin with such despair in my heart that I could hardly walk.

Suddenly her voice from high above: 'Paul ...' She was standing on a small balcony facing the street. 'You forgot the beast ...' I turned back and climbed the stairs again. A flicker of hope kept me going. She met me halfway down, handed me 'the beast' and then kissed me with all passion, all tenderness. That little beast with one ear had saved us.

A few weeks later she came to live with me. We embraced at the airport, laughed and cried, lost in great ecstasy. Before she arrived she'd written: 'We shall be happy together, even if it's only for one beautiful morning in spring.' We were amazingly happy for a full month, but slowly this unworldly love started to choke us; the pressure of living up to this mysterious passion became too much.

A virus attacked my heart — probably the same virus that had visited me in India some years earlier — and I found myself under crisp, white sheets with people staring at me through the mist. A tube in my nose, a long needle in my arm. Elisabeth above me. Her tears falling on my face. We went to the North to find some sun and peace. The doctor told me to stay very quiet and still and not to excite myself. Even making love was dangerous. We made love as soon as we arrived and she conceived. Three months later she decided to leave and asked me to kiss my baby goodbye. I kissed her warm, soft belly and plunged into an immeasurable darkness.

On the day I thought my child would be born I planted a small tree in my backyard. Within a few years, this tree was the tallest in the neighbourhood. Grew with such devastating speed that we had to cut it down.

Ezra.

Five years later. It was Carnaval in Cologne when I first held my son. His silhouette appeared behind some frosted glass. Then Elisabeth pushed him into the room and closed the door. He was dressed in a red Indian outfit, his head crowned with feathers. His face so familiar.

'Who are you?', he said in German.

'A very old friend', I replied.

We watched one another carefully. He climbed onto my knee and touched my face. Ezra — my son. That mysterious temple within, within all of us, started to shake. A small earthquake rocked the foundations.

I went outside, stood on a balcony facing the street. Brass bands marched past, people wearing masks, floats with flower gardens and beautiful maidens. The deafening sounds drowned my cries. We went down into the street, watched the procession close by. Ezra was mesmerised by all the madness, the frenzy, the screaming crowds. It rained lollies from a passing car. Ezra caught some with one hand in the air, the other remained firmly glued to mine.

Ezra travelled the world with his mother, lived and grew up in many different places. We had sporadic contact, but I had nothing to do with his upbringing. These days I share much time and many interests with him. He has become a fine and dedicated writer. When he was twelve, Elisabeth brought him to Australia. She'd decided that he should know who his real father was. It wasn't an easy task, certainly not for Ezra. I knew he liked me, but would he accept me? Ezra thought that Elisabeth's ex-husband was his father. They were and still are very close. When Elisabeth told him, he stared at her in disbelief. It didn't make any sense. He was confused, couldn't believe this to be true.

The next day, I took him for a drive. We circled the lake in silence. The weather changed continuously, from hail to sharp bursts of sunshine. I finally stopped the car, turned the rear vision mirror and pressed my head against his. Together we stared at our reflection.

'I am your father. It's true. Look, we have the same chin, the same cheekbone. Your eyes are from the East, but we look alike.'

I held him tight, could feel his heart beat. The rain now came pouring down. In silence we drove on.

Suddenly he touched my hand and said softly: 'Yes, I believe you.'

Kyra

I first met my daughter's mother when she visited me with her boyfriend. Juliet was very young, very beautiful. She played a small part in *Inside Looking Out* and I was asked to be the best man at their wedding. The marriage didn't last long. I remained friends with her husband, but she vanished.

It takes a lot to persuade me to go the movies. Especially to one of those entertainment centres with their buckets of popcorn, franchise ice creams and pinball machines. My friend Bernie Eddy had decided we needed a break from our pre-production activities on *Kostas* and he had a film in mind that could be worth the trouble. I can't remember what film it was, but outside on the footpath in the middle of a large crowd, we met Juliet and her brother. She greeted us with great warmth. Before we went into different cinemas, we decided to meet again.

Within six months, I found myself standing in her parents' backyard, facing my minister friend Brian Heath, who pronounced us man and wife. I was thirty-nine, she was twenty-one and pregnant. I didn't have the slightest idea what would become of our lives. I was satisfied with the simple joy of being with her. Most stories one tries to tell are incompatible with what really happens. I can only hint at the peace and tranquillity the first year of our marriage brought. How can I explain that I enjoyed the routine of coming home, being welcomed, sharing a meal. Home life as such had always

Kyra.

eluded me. Now I found myself living the bourgeois life and enjoying it immensely. Impossible to comprehend in retrospect and at the time alarming to people who knew me.

Juliet had a miscarriage; but soon after she became pregnant again and gave birth to our child, a daughter. In homage to Nijinsky, I insisted on calling her Kyra. This is the name of Nijinsky's first daughter who is still alive. I saw my little girl come into this world and was utterly overcome. Water and blood — so much water and blood. Before and during her birth, I had Janet Baker singing Schubert lieder. There was an argument with a matron about this, but she couldn't stop me.

Even as a child, I had a morbid fascination with decay and death. As Gustave Flaubert wrote: 'I can never look at a face, without seeing the skull behind it. Never watch children, without seeing them grow wrinkled and old, never look at a naked woman without imagining her skeleton or her death.' Kyra's birth changed all that. I no longer saw the skull behind the face. Kyra gave me life and hope and brought an immense peace into my heart.

It was therefore devastating when the marriage failed. One day Juliet announced that she was leaving me, had her own growing up to do, that I was far too obsessed and was crushing her existence. Those few years of idle dreaming had come to an awful end. Yes, indeed, I'd just completed *Man of Flowers* and had neglected her, but certainly not our daughter. Later Juliet returned, but our mutual trust had gone.

Kyra and I came home one night to an empty house. She was only three or four, but realised that the marriage had no more future. We sat huddled together, facing this new emptiness. I heard a sob coming from my little girl, a deep sigh from within, a terrible pain. It was not the pain of that moment only. Her hurt was much larger. Then she put her arms firmly around my neck. We slept that night like two wounded animals in a deep black cave, sharing our confusing dreams of sadness. Somehow we managed those bitter first years.

The family house was sold. Kyra and Juliet moved into a small place bought with the proceeds. I found myself on the road again. Starting afresh, moving from one place to another. A cheap motel near a railway line was my home during the making of *My First Wife*.

One day the laboratory informed us that something had gone wrong with the daily rushes. Tony Llewellyn-Jones and I returned to the production office to wait for more bad news. My life was in a mess. I was making a very demanding film. My financial situation was grim.

A few houses down from the office, an auction was taking place. A strange, U-shaped building, full of derelicts and retired prostitutes and within walking distance of the Bay. Tony and I watched the auctioneers and out of rage and frustration I put my hand up to make a bid. A little joke to raise our spirits. Suddenly all eyes were upon me, the bidding had stopped. The auctioneers went inside. I tried to walk away from the craziness. It had nothing to do with me. But all the blood had rushed to my feet. I couldn't move.

The auctioneers returned. 'We are here to sell'. Those were the last words I heard before someone shook my hand.

'Congratulations'.

The short walk back to the office, followed by the auctioneers was like my last moment on earth before the hangman put his noose around my neck. I think I tried to hold Tony's hand, needed support. He kept reassuring me that we'd be all right.

'We're in this together', he said.

I signed a cheque for ten per cent with no money in the bank. Had until Monday to save my life. The auctioneers, or rather executioners, congratulated me once again and left with the cheque. We returned to the set to continue the film. With the help of Jim

Khong we found the money and even managed to have a look inside the building.

We had bought the building for a song, but that only dawned on me much later. We didn't realise that this place would become a centre of great cinematographic activity. People, known and unknown, from all over the world, would come to visit. Young aspiring filmmakers were always welcome.

I realised that this was the best thing that had ever happened to me. Our new headquarters had enough room for Illumination Films and much space for living. A fresh light had appeared out of nowhere. Kyra and I had a new home. My partners, Tony Llewellyn-Jones and James Khong, also moved in upstairs. We lived in separate flats like dedicated monks. It was easier to access the telex machine in the early hours that way … and the early trams would wake us should we sleep too long.

When Kyra was ten, she left this little note.

> Dear daddy,
> I worry about you at times. The love I have for you will never die. I feel a strong bond between our opposite souls. I kneed [sic] you more than life itself. My father, your love for me that I cherish, shall never fade. Please, help me to understand life. Look after me daddy, never let me go.
>
> Your heart and soul,
>
> Kyroushka
>
> P.S. You never have to feel lonely, daddy. I'm always there for you.

Kyra is now a wonderful young woman. We're still learning much about life. That strong bond between our opposite souls is the greatest source of inspiration in my life.

Marius

To live a normal life is easy, but to be totally alive at all times is very difficult. Happiness should be called contentment, but how can one be totally alive when one is content? Art is probably the most unselfish form of happiness in the world, but the artist has to be strong — have the strength to stand up to a blow that would kill an ordinary person.

Strindberg thought that happiness and joy were for fools.

> ... the way people generally celebrate the joy of life as though joy consists in behaving idiotically and portraying the world as though it were peopled by lunatics with an insatiable passion for dancing. I find the joy of life in life's cruel and mighty conflicts. I delight in knowledge and discovery ...

The mother of my third child, Marius, is a gifted artist. A fine writer with a sharp intellect. We were unsuited, but recognised the artist soul in one another and shared a great passion for music. We were supremely alive in very small, amazing bursts.

Our relationship was extreme. The child that emerged from this, Marius, just had to be there, but he didn't make it easy for us. Anna wrote a book, *Stories from the Motherland*, about her years of captivity. A penetrating book of short stories which keeps me on the outside — watching her and Marius from behind a fence.

When Anna was pregnant, we went to Cannes. She felt even more alienated in the frenzy of Cannes than I did. Basically she was on her own and I was out attending meetings and talking to people. Anna had taken up knitting and had produced one large, long shawl. The shawl had started rather wide and grew narrower as the work progressed.

One evening I returned to our hotel and found Anna lying in bed, knitting at an alarming pace. The shawl was hitting the two

Marius.

meter mark in length, but the width by now was only a few inches. I had been testing the wine a bit too much and peacefully snuggled up to her. 'How was your day?' Unfortunately I fell asleep during her lengthy answer, then suddenly flew out of bed with a piercing pain in my back. In the mirror I saw that one of her needles was stuck under my shoulder blade. This was no time to lean against the wall. Later we both realised the absurdity of the situation.

We managed to get back to Australia and I started to work on *Golden Braid*. In the middle of the shoot, when Anna was eight months pregnant, I had to fly to Italy to attend a retrospective of my films. This was a long-standing promise. As soon as I arrived, I received the amazing news that Anna had given birth to a son. Within three days I was back again, went straight from the airport to the hospital and held mother and son. It had been an extremely difficult birth. Anna was exhausted. I was exhausted. The child almost died.

That same day I had to continue filming. We were behind schedule, of course. It was a lonely and devastating time for Anna. Her little boy was so perfect but the relationship was painfully off track. When I look back now I can see more clearly her painful situation and the lack of support she experienced.

Marius didn't have a name for many months. He was called 'the child'. We were the actual children. But humour saved us and has helped us to forgive and give him two parents who adore and love him. He actually has three parents, with Anna's husband, Peter, being a wonderful balance between us.

One of my father's brothers was a Benedictine monk who'd spent most of his life in a monastery, singing Gregorian hymns. After many years of solitude the remaining monks were sent into the world to become ordinary priests. This particular monk was called Marius. Uncle Marius could only communicate through song. This 'melodious training' made it impossible for him to hold a normal conversation. Everything he tried to say finished up as a chant, which amused everyone enormously. He was definitely on another planet — absent-minded, terribly kind and gentle. Uncle Marius was the celebrant at my sister Elizabeth's wedding and when he sang her praises, my youngest sister, Christa, who was the bridesmaid, became hysterical with laughter and urinated all over the altar.

This dear man had just died when we were looking for a name. Our child carries his name now. Marius lives on. The new Marius has shown a remarkable talent for music, loves singing and paints pictures of giant birds sitting in tiny trees. He's also terribly kind and gentle. He's teaching us much about the past and how to hold hands to face the future.

> *We are all pilgrims in this world.*
> *We come from afar, and we are going afar.*

I still wander the world. Sometimes I know where I'm going. Sometimes I don't. I still dream about a home, about a homecoming. The questions remain. The outward journey is painful, often more than flesh and blood can bear. The inward journey is rich and beautiful and deeply rewarding.

Some five years ago I revisited the house of my youth, my old family home. Time has collapsed here, images linger ... The house has been empty. Nobody has inhabited this place for well over two years, and everything has been left the way it was. Now I feel that terrible shyness again and the fear of coming home ... putting my arm through the small window in the door to open it. As soon as my hand goes into the dark, I feel the anxiety creeping up my arm and paralysing my body.

Injuries of our childhood last a lifetime. Age becomes an accumulation of scars. The secret of human existence does not consist merely in living, but in what one lives for. I desperately try to find an optimistic note but everything is closing in. Why did I come here?. I can't recall the details of our lives. They've disappeared into the abyss.

The old television set plays only one station. It happens to be a Russian orchestra playing Mozart's Fourth Violin Concerto. The camera cuts to large close-ups of the audience. Eisenstein hasn't been forgotten. Most of the people are crying. Russia has an enormous soul. I cry with them, feel totally depleted of all hope, all future. I remember August Strindberg's defence of his characters:

> These characters are agglomerations of past and present cultures, scraps from books and newspapers, fragments of humanity, torn shreds of one's fine clothing that has become rags, in just the way that a human soul is patched together.

Why Strindberg, right here? This is my past, the past that links up with my private, small world, with my children, my friends who have given me some peace and creativity. The world 'out there' is full of trepidation, but now this trepidation has crept into this house. We can never attempt an escape.

This morning I felt that all pain and sorrow had rolled themselves into a little pill and I had swallowed it. In the Middle Ages whole towns and villages went mad. An epidemic of madness, waves of collective insanity, affected the people. My life now feels like that. A collective act of madness, or rather a collection of mad acts.

There is my mother's worn-out chair and the couch on which she died. Some faded photographs on the dresser. A picture my mother always cherished is falling out of its frame. Her children, three years into the war, clutching at their dolls. I've already found comfort sucking on a pipe. The badly-stained carpet with markings of a lifetime. All those years, all those dreams, all that pain and confusion. Life is chaos but there's something logical and humane in memories. I've looked through the family documents. Poems my father wrote before and during the Second World War. My mother's letters and her housekeeping notes. She always hid the fact that there was no money, hardly enough to feed her children, to keep them alive.

I find some paintings my mother collected when we were children. Why do children paint and then stop painting when they reach 'thought'? There's also a rather comical letter from a school

Injuries of our childhood last a lifetime.

psychiatrist regarding 'Little Paul'. I have no recollection of this interview.

> Little Paul is a strange boy, obviously not too advanced. He doesn't seem to have the same intelligent spirit as your other children ... The best we can hope for is to find something he can do with his hands ... Keep encouraging him, though, but don't expect too much ...

No wonder my father treated me with a fair degree of suspicion!

My father's poems speak of the sky, of tenderness and hope, of the great massacre of the Second World War, of bombs, terror and death. One poem is called: 'The Sky is Red'. My mother writes: 'I hope that after the war we will have some peaceful years with our children'. Dear mother ... *lieve moeder*. A few years before she died she told me that there hadn't been one day without tears.

I've sat here all night. Early morning light is coming through the unseen window. A strange pale light without shadows. And I suddenly wonder whether my mother might not actually be happy now, that my father has found peace. The light changes. Patches of colour appear. They travel slowly on the wooden floor then merge with the carpet. I sense the world beyond the room. It is beautiful. But now, I've become a stranger here ... an outsider ... Everything is still hidden and hidden and hidden.

Filmography

MATUTA
1965 / 23 min. / 16mm

TIME PAST
1966 / 10 min. / 16mm

SKINDEEP
1968 / 40 min. / 16mm

MARCEL
1969 / 7 min. / 16mm

SYMPHONY
1969 / 12 min. / 16mm

MIRKA
1970 / 20 min. / 16mm

CALCUTTA
1970 / 30 min. / 16mm
Documentary

PHYLLIS
1971 / 35 min. / 16 mm

THE JOURNEY
1972 / 60 min. / 16 mm
CAST: Alan Money, Norman Kaye
Synopsis
A man travels back into his past, while being persecuted by a woman.

ALL SET BACKSTAGE
1974 / 22 min. / 16mm
Documentary

WE ARE ALL ALONE MY DEAR
1975 / 22 min. / 16mm

ISLAND
1975 / 10 min. / 16mm

ILLUMINATIONS
1976 / 78 min. / 16mm
Feature
DIRECTOR: Paul Cox
SCRIPT : Paul Cox
CAMERA: Paul Cox, Bryan Gracey
EDITOR: Paul Cox, Russell Hurley
PRODUCER: Tibor Markus
CAST: Gabriella Trsek, Tony Llewellyn-Jones, Norman Kaye, Alan Money, Sheila Florance, Athol Shmith
Synopsis
A woman returns from her father's funeral and tries to share her 'illuminations' with her lover.

INSIDE LOOKING OUT
1977 / 90 min. / 35mm
Feature
DIRECTOR: Paul Cox
SCRIPT: Paul Cox, Susan Holly Jones
CAMERA: Paul Cox
EDITORS: Paul Cox, Russell Hurley
MUSIC: Norman Kaye
PRODUCER: Paul Cox, Bernard Eddy
CAST: Briony Behets, Tony Llewellyn-Jones, Norman Kaye, Elke Neidhart, Juliet Bacskai, Dani Eddy
Synopsis
The film analyses the conventions and hypocrisy of a modern marriage.

WAYS OF SEEING
1977 / 24 min. / 16mm

RITUAL
1978 / 10 min. / 16mm

KOSTAS
1978 / 100 min. / 35 mm
Feature
DIRECTOR: Paul Cox
SCRIPT: Linda Aronson
CAMERA: Vittorio Bernini
EDITOR: John Scott
THEME MUSIC: Mikis Theodorakis, sung

by Margretha Zorbala
ASSOCIATE PRODUCER: Tony Llewellyn-Jones
PRODUCER: Bernard Eddy
CAST: Takis Emmanuel, Wendy Hughes, Tony Llewellyn-Jones
Synopsis
A love story in which a Greek and an Australian struggle with the barriers of their cultural differences. It is set against the background of Melbourne's Greek community and the lifestyle of an Anglo-Saxon divorcee.

FOR A CHILD CALLED MICHAEL
1979 / 30 min. / 16mm
Docu-Drama
DIRECTOR: Paul Cox
SCRIPT: Paul Cox
CAMERA: Vittorio Bernini
EDITOR: John Scott
PRODUCER: Illumination Films
CAST: Wendy Hughes, Chris Haywood

THE KINGDOM OF NEK CHAND
1980 / 22 min. / 16mm
Documentary
DIRECTOR: Paul Cox
SCRIPT: Ulli Beier
CAMERA: Paul Cox
EDITORS: Paul Cox, Ulli Beier
PRODUCER: Paul Cox, Bryan Gracey

UNDERDOG
1980 / 53 min. / 16mm
Documentary
DIRECTOR: Paul Cox
CAMERA: Paul Cox
EDITOR: Paul Cox
PRODUCER: Robert Calwill

LONELY HEARTS
1981/ 95 min. / 35mm
Feature
DIRECTOR: Paul Cox
SCRIPT: Paul Cox, John Clarke
CAMERA: Yuri Sokol, ACS
ART DIRECTOR: Neil Angwin
SOUND RECORDIST: Ken Hammond
EDITOR: Tim Lewis
MUSIC: Norman Kaye
EXECUTIVE PRODUCER: Phillip Adams
PRODUCER: John B. Murray
ASSOCIATE PRODUCERS: Erwin Rado, Fran Haarsma
CAST: Wendy Hughes, Norman Kaye, Jon Finlayson, Julia Blake, Jonathan Hardy
Synopsis
Returning to his gloomy family home after his mother's funeral Peter Thompson suddenly confronts his loneliness, and decides to embark upon an adventure. He goes to a lonely heart's club and pays for an introduction . He meets Patricia, also a victim of a smothering family; their first meeting requires some courage. Painfully shy and sexually inhibited, she becomes traumatised by his first clumsy attempt at love-making. After a series of grotesque episodes the couple establish a tentative friendship.

MAN OF FLOWERS
1983 / 91 min. / 35mm
Feature
DIRECTOR: Paul Cox
SCRIPT: Paul Cox, DIALOGUE: Bob Ellis
CAMERA: Yuri Sokol, ACS
OPERATOR: Nino Martinetti
SOUND RECORDIST: Lloyd Carrick
ART DIRECTOR: Asher Bilu
EDITOR: Tim Lewis
MUSIC: excerpts from Donizetti's *Lucia di Lammermoor* with Jose Carreras and Montsarrat Caballe
EXECUTIVE PRODUCER: William T. Marshall
PRODUCER: Jane Ballantyne, Paul Cox
ASSOCIATE PRODUCER: Tony Llewellyn-Jones
CAST: Norman Kaye, Alyson Best, Chris Haywood, Sarah Walker

Synopsis
Charles Bremer is a recluse and collector of rare flowers and objets d'art. Each Wednesday he takes Lisa, an artist's model, to his sumptuous house and pays her to strip to the love duet from Donizetti's *Lucia di Lammermoor*. Lisa, his little flower, introduces him to the world of David Saunders — an old fashioned action painter and a new threat to Charles's world.

DEATH AND DESTINY: A JOURNEY INTO ANCIENT EGYPT
1984 / 120 min. / 16mm
Documentary
DIRECTOR: Paul Cox
SCRIPT: Michael le Moignan, Phillip Adams, Paul Cox
CAMERA: Yuri Sokol, ACS
OPERATOR: James Grant
EDITORS: John Scott, Paul Cox
PRODUCER: Will Davies

MY FIRST WIFE
1984 / 97 min. / 35mm
Feature
DIRECTOR: Paul Cox
SCRIPT: Paul Cox,
SCREEN ADAPTATION: Paul Cox, Bob Ellis
CAMERA: Yuri Sokol, ACS
OPERATOR: Nino Martinetti
SOUND RECORDIST: Ken Hammond
ART DIRECTOR: Asher Bilu
EDITOR: Tim Lewis
EXECUTIVE PRODUCER: William T. Marshall
PRODUCER: Jane Ballantyne, Paul Cox
ASSOCIATE PRODUCER: Tony Llewellyn-Jones
CAST: John Hargreaves, Wendy Hughes, Lucy Angwin, David Cameron
Synopsis
Helen has decided to leave the marriage and it is John who lacks the inner resources to cope with the impending tragedy. Slowly he is sucked into a tunnel of despair — fighting his conservative nature and the romantic memories of his married life. The film pleads for more tolerance and understanding of our loved ones, and, if the time for parting arrives, more care in the way we say goodbye.

PAPER BOY
1985 / 53 min. / 16mm
Children's television film
DIRECTOR: Paul Cox
SCRIPT: Bob Ellis
CAMERA: Yuri Sokol, ACS
OPERATOR: Michael Edols
SOUND RECORDIST: Andrew Ramage
PRODUCTION DESIGNER: Neil Angwin
EDITOR: Tim Lewis
COSTUME DESIGNER: Jennie Tate
PRODUCTION MANAGER: Robert Kewley
PRODUCER: Jane Ballantyne
SUPERVISING PRODUCER: Jeff Peck
EXECUTIVE PRODUCER: Patricia Edgar
CAST: Christopher Schlusser, Tony Llewellyn-Jones, Linden Wilkinson, Norman Kaye, David Argue, John Duigan
Synopsis
In 1932 11-year-old Joe Riordan becomes his family's sole means of support when his father gets the sack. When he and his father have a disagreement, Joe leaves home and begins a hard battle for survival on the streets. At a belated Christmas celebration the family is reconciled.

HANDLE WITH CARE
1985 / 75 min. / 16mm
Documentary
DIRECTOR: Paul Cox
SCRIPT: Anne Brooksbank
CAMERA: Yuri Sokol, ACS
EDITOR: Tim Lewis
PRODUCER: Andrena Finlay, Annika Landa
CAST: Anna Maria Monticelli, Nina Landis, Monica Maughan, Peter Adams

CACTUS
1986 / 95 min. / 35mm
Feature
DIRECTOR: Paul Cox
SCREENPLAY: Paul Cox, Bob Ellis, Norman Kaye
SCENARIO: Paul Cox,
ADDITIONAL DIALOGUE: Morris Lurie
CAMERA: Yuri Sokol, ACS
OPERATOR: Nino Martinetti
SOUND RECORDIST: Ken Hammond
PRODUCTION DESIGNER: Asher Bilu
EDITOR: Tim Lewis
EXECUTIVE PRODUCER: Jeannine Seawell, William T. Marshall
PRODUCER: Jane Ballantyne, Paul Cox
ASSOCIATE PRODUCER: Tony Llewellyn-Jones
CAST: Isabelle Huppert, Robert Menzies, Norman Kaye, Monica Maughan
Synopsis
Colo, a French woman holidaying in Australia has her sight critically damaged in a car accident. Without resources to cope with the impending tragedy she begins to withdraw from the world until she meets Robert, a blind lecturer at a training school for the blind. As their relationship develops, both Colo and Robert become aware of deeper dimensions in their lives and Colo's growing love for the blind man totally changes her understanding of 'sight'.

THE SECRET LIFE OF TREES
1986 / 25 min. / 16mm
Children's television film
DIRECTOR: Paul Cox
SCRIPT: Paul Cox
CAMERA: Brendan Lavelle
ART DIRECTOR: Neil Angwin, Victoria Rowell, Viv Wilson
EDITOR: Russell Hurley
PRODUCER: Tony Llewellyn-Jones
SUPERVISING PRODUCER: Jeff Peck
EXECUTIVE PRODUCER: Patricia Edgar
CAST: Lucy Angwin, Ramesh Prevot, David Alexander
Synopsis
In a dream a little girl is called by the trees outside her bedroom window to come and visit. She is surprised to find she can 'enter' the trees and here, inside mysterious tunnels and caverns she meets a series of wonderful characters, representing the interior ecological system of the trees. The film has a pointed morality in its parallels between the exterior and interior of trees and that of human beings.

VINCENT, THE LIFE AND DEATH OF VINCENT VAN GOGH
1987/ 95 min./ 35 mm
Feature
DIRECTOR: Paul Cox
SCRIPT: Paul Cox, based on the letters of Vincent van Gogh
CAMERA: Paul Cox
SECOND UNIT: Nino Martinetti
EDITOR: Paul Cox
PRODUCTION CO-ORDINATOR: Brendan Lavelle
EXECUTIVE PRODUCER: Klaus Selinger
PRODUCER: Tony Llewellyn-Jones
With the voice of John Hurt as Vincent van Gogh
Synopsis
The film tells the story of Vincent van Gogh through his letters to his brother Theo, from 1872 until the time of his death. With these records we gain some insight into the man, his motivations and his unique humanity. Through his own words the film explores the Europe Vincent explored, the sites of his inspiration and the colours and seasons he experienced, from Groot-Zundert, Neunen, the Borinage, the Hague, Paris, Arles and St. Remy to Auvers, where he died.

THE GIFT
1988 / 90 min. / 16mm
Children's television film
DIRECTOR: Paul Cox
SCRIPT: Paul Cox, Jeff Peck, based on a story by Georgina Beier.
CAMERA: Nino Martinetti
PRODUCTION DESIGNER: Paul Ammitzboll
EDITOR: Russell Hurley
MUSIC: Tassos Ioannides
ASSOCIATE PRODUCER: Geoff Daniels
SUPERVISING PRODUCER: Jeff Peck
EXECUTIVE PRODUCER: Patricia Edgar
PRODUCER: Tony Llewellyn-Jones
CAST: Nicholas Hatjiandreou, Vicky Serbos, Alexis Anthopoulos, Con Laras, Rena Frangioudakis
Synopsis
When two Greek-Australian children from an inner Melbourne suburb win first prize in a national lottery, their prize — 500 hectares of 'beautiful bushland' in Western Australia — becomes the object of a family dispute. Nikos and Sophia travel across the Nullarbor with their grandfather to see their prize unaware that, back in Melbourne, their father has agreed to sell the trees on the newly won land to raise money to buy a new house.

ISLAND
1989 / 95 min. / 35mm
Feature
DIRECTOR: Paul Cox
SCRIPT: Paul Cox
ASSISTANT DIRECTOR: Paul Ammitzboll
CAMERA: Michael Edols
SOUND RECORDIST AND MIXER: James Currie
PRODUCTION DESIGNER: Neil Angwin
EDITOR: John Scott
MUSIC by Rabindranath Tagore, sung by Rita Guha
EXECUTIVE PRODUCER: William T. Marshall, Jeannine Seawell
PRODUCER: Paul Cox, Santhana Naidu
ASSOCIATE PRODUCER: Takis Emmanuel
CAST: Irene Papas, Chris Haywood, Eva Sitta, Anoja Weerasinghe
Synopsis
Three women — an Australian, a Sri Lankan, and a Greek — meet on a Greek island in the Dodecanese. All are exiles escaping from their own tragedies. Their lives become inextricably linked by their common desires and mutual fear of the outside world. Ultimately it is the island itself leads all three into revelations about themselves and their place in the world.

GOLDEN BRAID
1990 / 91 min. / 35mm
Feature
DIRECTOR: Paul Cox
SCRIPT: Paul Cox, Barry Dickins
CAMERA: Nino Martinetti, ACS
SOUND RECORDIST AND MIXER: James Currie
PRODUCTION DESIGNER: Neil Angwin
EDITOR: Russell Hurley
EXECUTIVE PRODUCER: William T. Marshall
PRODUCERS: Paul Cox, Paul Ammitzboll, Santhana Naidu
CAST: Chris Haywood, Gosia Dobrowolska, Paul Chubb, Norman Kaye, Marion Heathfield
Synopsis
Bernard is a clock-maker with a passion for antiques. One day in the secret panel of a cabinet he finds a marvellous braid of golden hair. He associates the braid with his own past, distances himself from his lover Terese, and finally falls in love with it. An erotic comedy based on a Guy de Maupassant short story

A WOMAN'S TALE
1991/ 93 min. / 35mm
Feature
DIRECTOR: Paul Cox

SCRIPT: Paul Cox, Barry Dickins
CAMERA: Nino Martinetti, ACS
SOUND RECORDIST AND MIXER: James Currie
PRODUCTION DESIGNER: Neil Angwin
EDITOR: Russell Hurley
MUSIC: Paul Grabowsky
EXECUTIVE PRODUCER: William T. Marshall
LINE PRODUCER: Paul Ammitzboll
PRODUCER: Paul Cox, Santhana Naidu
CAST: Sheila Florance, Gosia Dobrowolska, Norman Kaye, Chris Haywood, Myrtle Woods, Ernest Gray

Synopsis
At almost eighty years of age, Martha has seen the good and the bad, and now offers her love and wisdom to all who are willing to listen to her. Her closest ally is Anna, her district nurse, who understands Martha's independent spirit. Her son and the authorities decide it's time for her to be committed to a home for the aged. But Martha has other plans.

THE NUN AND THE BANDIT
1992 / 92 min. / 35mm
Feature
DIRECTOR: Paul Cox
SCRIPT: Paul Cox, based on the book by E.L. Grant Watson
CAMERA: Nino Martinetti, ACS
SOUND RECORDIST AND MIXER: James Currie
PRODUCTION DESIGNER: Neil Angwin
EDITOR: Paul Cox
MUSIC: Tommy Lewis
EXECUTIVE PRODUCER: William T. Marshall
PRODUCER: Paul Cox, Paul Ammitzboll
CAST: Gosia Dobrowolska, Chris Haywood, Victoria Eagger, Charlotte Hughes Haywood, Norman Kaye, Tom E. Lewis, Scott Michael Stephenson, Robert Menzies, Eva Sitta

Synopsis
Left without a mother and mistreated by their father, Michael Shanley and his brothers become a law unto themselves. One day, after a fruitless visit to their well-to-do Uncle George, Michael persuades his brothers to help him kidnap their fourteen-year-old second cousin and hold her for ransom. The girl is being chaperoned by a visiting nun, who refuses to abandon her charge. Michael loses his sense of perspective and falls in love with the nun, unleashing a psychological tug of war between the two.

TOUCH ME
1993 / 26 min. / 35mm
Episode 'Erotic Tales'
DIRECTOR: Paul Cox
SCRIPT: Paul Cox, Barry Dickins, Margot Wiburd
CAMERA: Nino Martinetti, ACS
SOUND RECORDIST: James Currie, Craig Carter
ART DIRECTION: Neil Angwin
EDITOR: Paul Cox
EXECUTIVE PRODUCER: Regina Ziegler
LINE PRODUCER: Illumination Films
PRINCIPAL CAST: Gosia Dobrowolska, Claudia Karvan, Chris Haywood, Barry Otto, David Field, Norman Kaye

EXILE
1994 / 96 min. / 35mm
Feature
DIRECTOR: Paul Cox
SCRIPT: Paul Cox, based on the book *Priest Island* by E.L. Grant Watson
CAMERA: Nino Martinetti, ACS
SOUND RECORDIST AND MIXER: James Currie
EDITOR: Paul Cox
MUSIC: Paul Grabowsky
PRODUCTION DESIGNER: Neil Angwin
COSTUME DESIGNER: Gosia Dobrowolska
EXECUTIVE PRODUCER: William T. Marshall
PRODUCER: Santhana Naidu, Paul

Ammitzboll, Paul Cox
CAST: Aden Young, Beth Champion, Claudia Karvan, David Field, Norman Kaye, Chris Haywood, Nicholas Hope, Tony Llewellyn-Jones, Barry Otto, Hugo Weaving, Gosia Dobrowolska
Synopsis
Late last century the sentence of banishment to an island was passed on a young man whose only crime was to steal a few sheep in order to secure the dowry for the girl he loved. Haunted by his lost love, he fights the demons of his past and the ghosts of his present until he slowly learns how to live off land and sea. A girl from the mainland learns of Peter's isolated existence and, compelled by her own loneliness and her romantic dreams, decides to join him on the island.

LUST AND REVENGE
1996 / 90 min./ 35 mm
Feature
DIRECTOR: Paul Cox
SCRIPT: Paul Cox, John Clarke
CAMERA: Nino Martinetti, ACS
sound recordist and mixer: James Currie
PRODUCTION DESIGNER: Neil Angwin
EDITOR: John Scott
MUSIC: Paul Grabowsky, sung by Maya Damayanthi, Kushani Damayanthi
EXECUTIVE PRODUCER: William T. Marshall
PRODUCTION MANAGER: David Lightfoot
PRODUCER: Paul Cox, Jane Ballantyne
CAST: Nicholas Hope, Gosia Dobrowolska, Claudia Karvan, Victoria Eagger, Chris Haywood, Norman Kaye, Ulli Birve, Robert Menzies, Bryan Dawe, John Hargreaves, Max Gillies, Wendy Hughes, Pamela Rabe, Paul Cox, Eva Hamburg, John Larkin
Synopsis
The mischievous heiress Georgina, decides to commission her friend Lily, an internationally recognised sculptress, to create a work in the vein of Michelangelo's 'David'. The over-religious wife of the model becomes jealous of the attention her husband is receiving. At the height of the sessions the erratic Georgina slips the wife a powerful aphrodisiac. In this erotic satire all the characters are seeking love and yet all are manipulated and exploited.

THE HIDDEN DIMENSION
1997 / 45 min. / IMAX 3-D
DIRECTOR: Paul Cox
SCRIPT: Barbara Kerr, John Larkin, Margot Wiburd, Paul Cox, Marc Strange
CAMERA: Vic Sarin
PRODUCERS: Sally Dundas, Barbara Kerr, Lorne Orleans
EXECUTIVE PRODUCER IN CHARGE: Andrew Gellis,
EXECUTIVE PRODUCERS: Dennis B. Kane, Jonathan Barker
EDITOR: Barbara Kerr
SOUND RECORDIST: James Currie
SOUND MIXER: Peter Thillaye
MUSIC: Richard Robbins
CAST: Charlotte Sullivan, Gosia Dobrowolska, C. David Johnson, with the voice of James Garner
Synopsis
Eleven-year-old Elly travels with her parents to her grandfather's country house while he's away on a research trip. She spends her days exploring the rambling home and soon discovers that her grandfather, an eccentric inventor, has left her a treasure map of sorts. The Hidden Dimension refers to the millions of microscopic life forms which share our lives as another universe. IMAX technology reveals this microcosm of daily life and the film leaves us with the message that we must use our eyes and our curiosity to honour the mysteries of nature and see more deeply into life.

Retrospectives

1984	HOF International Film Festival
	Tribute to Paul Cox
1984	Toronto Film Festival
	'10 Filmmakers for the Future'
1986	Dutch Film Festival (Utrecht)
1986	Ghent International Film Festival
	Homage to Paul Cox
1986	Telluride Film Festival
	Retrospective
1987	American Film Institute
	Retrospective
1987	Denver Film Festival
	Tribute to Paul Cox
1988	Olympic Film Festival (Calgary)
	Retrospective
1989	Sulmona Cinema Festival (Italy)
	Retrospective
1990	Calcutta International Film Festival
	Retrospective
1992	Istanbul International Film Festival
	Retrospective
1992	Une semaine Internationale du Cinema (Tokyo)
1992	Film Society of Lincoln Center (New York)
	Retrospective

1992	Film Critics' Circle of Australia Tribute to Paul Cox
1993	Bombay — New Dehli — Calcutta — Madras Retrospective
1993	Brisbane International Film Festival Chauvel Award
1994	Dutch Film Festival (Utrecht) Cinema Militant Lecture
1994	Museum of Modern Art at Heide (Australia) A Festival of Films by Paul Cox
1995	Cape Town Film Festival Retrospective
1996	*A Journey with Paul Cox* (Belgium) Documentary by Gerrit Messiaen and Robert Visser
1997	International Film Festival of Brussels Retrospective
1997	*Ein Fremder in der Welt* (Germany) Documentary by Alexander Bohr for ZDF/ARTE

INDEX

Abraham, John, 95
Acharya, Anil, 90
Adams, Phillip, 153, 172
AFI *see* Australian Film Institute
altar boy, experience as, 25–26
Ammitzboll, Paul, 139, 165, 168, 175
Angeline (sister), 46, 159, 161
Angwin, Neil, 165
Antonioni, Michelangelo, 172
Aravindan (holy man of Kerala), 95
army, conscription into, 48–49
arrest and jail, 80–82
art school, attendance at, 49
audience, 122, 125
Australia
    departure from, 58
    early months, 56–58
    first impressions, 55–56
    journey to, 53–54
    land and people, distinction between, 83
    love for, 83
    photographic studio, 63
    return to, 62
Australian Ballet, commissions by, 68
Australian Film Institute (AFI)
    Best Actress Award, 177
    Best Film Award, 172
Australian Human Rights Award, 176

Babenco, Hector, 148
Baillieu, Marianne, 63, 83, 157
Ballantyne, Jane, 153, 188
Barnes, Ethel, 70–73
Beath, Linda, 159
beauty, 114–115
Beier, Georgina, 70
Beier, Ulli, 70, 111, 189
Benders, Harry, 49

Benegal, Shyam, 95
Beresford, Bruce, 188
Bergman, Ingmar, 87, 150, 172
Best, Alyson, 156
Best Actress Award (AFI), 177
Best Film Award (AFI), 172
Bhagavadgita, The, 87
Bilu, Asher, 153, 154, 160
Bilu, Luba, 154
birth, 31, 32
Birve, Ulli, 187
Blake, Julia, 169
Born Innocent, 126
Boys in the Band, The, 72
Bunuel, Luis, 172, 173

Cactus, 20, 31, 101, 107–108, 126, 127, 157
Calcutta, 95–98
    documentary, 95–96
    images of, 99–100
camera salesman, job as, 56
Campbell, Jean, 73
Camus, Albert, 49
Cannes Film Festival, 156, 157, 202
    Man of Flowers, screening of, 156
    Vincent, screening of, 161
Cape Town Film Festival, 142
car accident, 62
Castle, The, 49
Cato, John, 74
Champion, Beth, 185
Chand, Nek, 111–112
Chatwin, Bruce, 157, 158
childhood memories, 35–36, 206–207
    Christmas, 45
    death of bird, 38
    films, 7, 83
    forest, light and sound in, 20–22

home, 36–37
post war period, 14–16
Queen Wilhelmina, visit by, 35
religious instruction, 26–27
school, 16–18, 40
sense of doom, 43
sleepwalking, 19
women's breasts, 18–19
World War II, 11–13
China, film festival in, 146–148
Christa (sister), 46, 204
Clarke, John, 185
Clement, René, 88
Comfort, Millie, 159
consumerism, 119–120, 141
Coumans, Willem, 62
Cox, Wim (father), 161
   death, 139–140
   marriage, 24
   obsessive behaviour, 43–44, 45
   poems, 207, 209
Cox–Kuminack, Else Amalia (mother)
   birth, 24
   grave, 22
   marriage, 24
   sight, loss of, 101
creative process, 8–9, 72–73, 173
Crowley, Mart, 72
Currie, Jim, 168, 184

Dasgupta, Buddhadeb, 95
Davidson, Ian, 153
Davies, Elsa, 73
Dawe, Bryan, 187
De Chirico, Giorgio, 189
Delhi Film Festival, 93–94
De–Marchi, Maria, 73
Diary of Vaslav Nijinsky, The, 64, 66–67
Dickins, Barry, 174
Dobrowolska, Gosia, 138, 139, 175, 177, 187, 190
documentary on Calcutta, 95–96
Don Quixote, still photographer for, 68, 150
Douglas, Michael, 159
dreams, stories and magic moments, 105–107, 206

Auschwitz, visit to, 135
Auvers–sur–Oise, visit to, 131–132
childhood home, 137–138
China, visit to, 146–148
dolphins, 130–131
Eastern Europe, railway station in, 134
Greece, night in, 135
hotels in foreign cities, 134–135
New York, meeting in, 132–134
Niagara Falls, visit to, 141–142
old woman, making love with, 136
parking lot, misplacing car in, 145–146
Shampoo Week in LA, 118–119
shooting a film, 138–139
smoking, 115–117
South Africa, visit to, 142–145
spring morning, 135–136
temple in Rome, 136–137

Eastwood, Clint, 125
Eddy, Bernie, 63–64, 197
Edols, Michael, 153, 166
Elippathayam, 95
Elizabeth (sister), 43, 46, 205
Ellis, Bob, 154, 157
Emmanual, Takis, 171
Empire of the Senses, 148
Exile, 142, 143
   making of, 181–185
Ezra (son), 173, 196–197

family photographic business, 19–20, 43, 46
   Studio 45, establishment of, 16
father *see* Cox, Wim
Fellini, Federico, 132, 172
Field, David, 185
film festivals
   Cannes *see* Cannes Film Festival
   Cape Town, 142
   China, 146–148
   Delhi, 93–94
   Ghent, 177
   Telluride *see* Telluride Film Festival
   Toronto, 162
   Utrecht, 31
   Vancouver, 162

Film Finance Corporation, 187
filmmaking, influences on *See also* influential films
   Arturo Toscanini, 83
   Bruce Chatwin, 157, 158
   Ingmar Bergman, 87
   Jacques Tati, 87
   music, 58
   painting, 110, 173, 189
   Serge Paradjanov, 72–73, 87
   Vaslav Nijinsky, 63–67
films
   early, 76–77, 84–86, 163
   European influence, 82
   funding *see* finance
   Hollywood, made in, 113–114, 120
   Indian cinema, 94–95
   influential *see* influential films
   reality, depiction of, 75–76
   reason for making, 120
   reviews, 156, 162, 163, 175, 177, 179, 188
   Super 8, 63
   television, effect of, 121
   violence in, 125–126
finance, 170–173
   federal, 171
   Lust and Revenge, 187–188
   Woman's Tale, A, 174–175
Fisher, Hannah, 162
Flaubert, Gustave, 199
Florance, Sheila, 20, 72–73, 174–178, 179
   AFI Best Actress, 177
Flowers International, establishment of, 153
Forbidden Games, 88
Force of Destiny, The, 83–84
Foster, Jodie, 129
France, 34
Frew, Bill, 77

Ghatak, Ritwik, 95
Ghent Film Festival, Grand Prix at, 177
Gide, André, 49
Godbold, David, 154
Gogh, Theo van, 163

Gogh, Vincent van, 8–9, 37, 57, 73, 75, 88–89, 105, 158
   film about *see Vincent, the Life and Death of Vincent van Gogh*
   grave, 131–132
Golden Braid, 204
Gopalakrishnan, Adoor, 95
Grabowsky, Paul, 175
Gration, Phyllis, 79
Greece, visit to, 163
   Island, making of, 163–169
Guha, Ritu, 90–91

Hargreaves, John, 157, 187
Haywood, Chris, 143, 153, 165–166, 169, 187
Healey, Joan, 63
Heath, Brian, 197
Helpmann, Robert, 67
Herzog, Lucki, 154
Herzog, Werner, 83, 153, 154, 157
Hidden Dimension, The, 189–191
Holland
   departure from, 53–54
   evacuation to north, 12–13
Hollywood filmmaking, 113–114, 120, 173
   conversations, 122–124
   criticism of, 127–128
Hollywood Reporter, review in, 163
Home of Man — The People of New Guinea, 70
Homecoming, 171
homesickness, 82
   film about, 84–86
Hope, Nicholas, 187
Hospital, Janette Turner, 185
Hughes, Wendy, 138, 157, 187
Human Still Lives from Nepal, 104–105
Hungary, crossing to, 39–40
Huppert, Isabelle, 20, 126, 127, 128, 129, 157
Hurley, Russell, 77
Hurt, John, 160–161
Hutton, Betty, 177

Illumination Films, purchase of

premises, 200–201
Illuminations, 67, 150
Im Kwon-Tack, 148
IMAX format, film made in *see Hidden Dimension, The*
India, 68
  experiences and impressions, 91–93
  film industry, 94–95
  hotel telephones, operation of, 101–104
  images, 32, 92, 96–97, 99–100, 101
  music, 90–91
  Rock Garden in Chandigarh, 111–112
influential films
  Forbidden Games, 88
  Monsieur Hulot's Holiday, 87
  Persona, 87
  Shadows of our Forgotten Ancestors, 72, 73, 87
Innocence, 188
Inside Looking Out, 197
Island, 30, 86, 90, 162
  early short film, 85–87, 163
  making of, 163–169
  poem, 85–86

Jaap (husband of Angeline), 159, 161
Jacoba (sister), 46
Jeux Interdits see Forbidden Games
Jewish Bride, The, 89
Johnson, C. David, 190
Journey, The, 76
  making of, 83–84, 85

Kafka, Franz, 49
Karate Kid, The, 127
Karvan, Claudia, 185
Kaye, Norman, 83, 138, 139, 149–150, 153, 169, 183
Kelly, Bill, 160
Kerr, Barbara, 190
Keys, Wendy, 178
Khong, Jim, 151, 200, 201
Kierkegaard, S.A., 49
Kieslowski, Krzysztof, 129
Kinnear, Rod, 77
Klingberg, Dawn, 174
Kostas, 151, 197

Kyra (daughter), 24, 107, 197–201
  Greece, visit to, 163

Lacemaker, The, 129
Langley, Robert, 77
Larkin, John, 138, 187, 190
Lavelle, Brendan, 59
Leiss, Elena, 73
L'Etranger, 49
L'Immoraliste, 49
Little Red Book, 147, 148
Llewellyn-Jones, Tony, 151, 153, 159, 161, 162, 200, 201
Loane, Barry, 188
Lonely Hearts, 83, 150, 153, 169, 172, 185
  AFI Best Film Award, 172
Loren, Sophia, 147
Los Angeles, experiences in, 115–119
Lowe, Don, 180–181
LSD, experiment with, 80–81
Lust and Revenge, 185–188
  finance, 187–188

Magnum Force, 125
Man of Flowers, 32, 82, 150, 151, 184, 199
  Cannes, screening at, 156
  flashbacks in, 18–19
  Lucia di Lammermoor, recording of, 154–155
  making of, 153–156
  reviews, 156
Mandela, Nelson, 143
Mao Zedong (Mao Tse-tung), 147, 148
Marius (son), 202–205
Marius (uncle), 204–205
Markus, Tibor, 67, 150–151
Marshall, Bill, 151, 153, 175
Martinetti, Nino, 166, 175
Matuta, 76, 77
McCann, Judith, 172, 185
Melbourne Film Festival, 22
Melbourne University, enrolment at, 58
Menzies, Robert, 157
Money, Alan, 84
Monsieur Hulot's Holiday, 87

mother *see* Cox–Kuminack, Else Amalia
movie "stars," attitude to, 120
music
   classical, 56–57
   film, influence on, 58
   India, of, 90–91
My First Wife, 157, 200

Naidu, Sonny, 175
Nepal, 104
   Annapurna, vision of, 32
   monastic experience, 108–110
Nijinsky, Romola, 64, 66
Nijinsky, Tamara, 66
Nijinsky, Vaslav, 57, 63–67, 73, 199
Nun and the Bandit, The, 93–94, 180–181
Nureyev, Rudolph, 67, 68, 72

Olivier, Lawrence, 83
Oshima, Nagisa, 147, 148

painting, inspiration from, 110, 173, 189
Palmer, Chris, 84
Palmer, Greta, 84
Palmer, Maudie, 78, 84
Papas, Irene, 30, 166, 169, 171
Paradjanov, Serge, 73
Paris, visit to, 50
Parr, Lenton, 74
Persona, 87
photography, 49–50, 60
   exhibitions, 62
   family business *see* family photographic business
   studio in Australia, 63
poems, 85–86, 109–110
   father, by, 207, 209
post war period, 14–15
Prahran College, work at
   lecturer in cinematography, 74
   photographic department, 74
Priest Island, 181
Pulp Fiction, 144

Rabe, Pamela, 187
Rado, Erwin, 22

Ray, Satyajit, 95
reincarnation, 100
relationships
   Anna, 202–204
   Carol, 58
   Elisabeth, 193–196
   Juliet, 197–200
religion
   instruction at school, 26–27
   thoughts on, 105
Rembrandt van Rijn, 89
Rilke, Rainer Maria, 177
Robocop, 125
Rogeon, Jean–François, 78

Sacrifice, The, 126, 127, 128
Sarris, Andrew, 162
Sartre, Jean–Paul, 49
Saul, John Ralston, 180
Schepisi, Fred, 188
school, 16–17, 40
Schwarz, Monique, 78
Scott, Jay, 161
Scott, John, 167
Seawell, Jeannine, 102–104, 187
Sen, Mrinal, 95
Shadows of our Forgotten Ancestors, 73, 87
Shaw, Bernard, 60
Shmith, Athol, 74
Silence of the Lambs, 126
Sitta, Eva, 169
sleepwalking, 19
smoking (a dialogue), 115–118
Social Snaps, job at, 56, 58
Sokol, Yuri, 153
Songlines, 158
Sopyonje, 148
South Africa, visit to, 142–145
South Australian Film Corporation, 172
Stone, Oliver, 147
Stories from the Motherland, 202
Stratton, David, 188
Streeton, Oliver, 160
Strindberg, August, 202, 206
Studio 45, establishment of, 16, 19–20
Suicide of a Gentleman, 185
Sullivan, Charlotte, 190

Sunflowers, 89
Super 8 films, 63

Tagore, Rabindranath, 57, 90, 99, 101
Tait, Lady Viola, 73
Takano, Etsuko, 179
Tammer, Peter, 78
Tarkovsky, Andrei, 120, 126, 127
Tati, Jacques, 87
Teen Werewolf, 127
Tel Aviv, 34
telephone call in India (a dialogue), 102–104
Telluride Film Festival, 126–129
  return to, 129
  speech at, 127–128
Ten Thousand Years in a Lifetime, 189
Theodorakis, Mikis, 171
Time Past, 77
Top Gun, 127, 128
Toronto Film Festival, 163, 180
Toscanini, Arturo, 83
travel
  Australia, to, 53–55
  China, 146–148
  French cargo boat, on, 58–59, 60
  Greece, 163
  India *see* India
  Indonesia, 68
  Nepal *see* Nepal
  New Guinea, 68–70
  South Africa, 142–145

Utrecht Film Festival, 31

van Gogh, Theo, 162
van Gogh, Vincent, *see* Gogh, Vincent van
Vancouver Film Festival, 162
Vandeputte, Alexander, 187
Variety, reviews in, 163, 188
Venlo, 31, 32
Verhoeven, Leonie, 31
Vermeer, Jan
  family relation to, 36
  paintings, 110–111, 189
Victorian Film Corporation, 165
Village Voice, review in, 163

Villon, François, 66
Vincent, the Life and Death of Vincent van Gogh, 66, 107, 158–163
  Australia, reception in, 162
  Cannes, screening at, 161
  Hollywood Reporter, review in, 163
  making of, 158–161
  New York, reception in, 163
  Toronto Film Festival, screening at, 162
  Vancouver Film Festival, screening at, 162
  Village Voice, review in, 163
violence in film, 125–126
Vivisector, The, 82
Voltaire's Bastards, 180
Voss, 82

Walker, Alice, 139
Watkins, Peter, 121, 139
Watson, Grant, 83, 180–181
Weaving, Hugo, 138, 187
Weerasinghe, Anoja, 162, 169
Weir, Peter, 188
Where the Green Ants Dream, 157
White, Patrick, 82–83
Wiburd, Margot, 190
Wilde, Oscar, 9
Wilson, Jim, 85
Wim (brother), 25, 161
  amateur acting, 27–28
  friendship, reawakening of, 39–40
Woman's Tale, A, 20, 72, 129, 142
  AFI Best Actress Award, 177
  finance, 174–175
  Grand Prix, Ghent Film Festival, 177
  Japan, screening in, 179
  making of, 174–178
  New York, screening in, 178–179
  New York Times, review in, 179
Woods, Myrtle, 73
World War II, 11–13
Wouters, Jean-Pierre, 156

Yeats, W.B., 57
Young, Aden, 185

Zorba the Greek, 151